THE END OF ECONOMIC GROWTH?

Growth and Decline in the UK since 1945

G. B. Stafford

Martin Robertson · Oxford

First published in 1981 by Martin Robertson & Company Ltd., 108 Cowley Road, Oxford OX4 1JF.

British Library Cataloguing in Publication Data

Stafford, Bernard
  The end of economic growth?
  1. Great Britain – Economic conditions – 1945-
  I. Title
  330.9′41′085   HC 256.5

  ISBN 0-85520-390-0
  ISBN 0-85520-396-X Pbk

Typeset in 11 on 12 pt VIP Times by Preface Ltd, Salisbury
Printed and bound in Great Britain by Book Plan, Worcester

Contents

iii

Introduction

Since the Second World War the UK has not achieved the rate of economic growth enjoyed by even the slowest-growing economy in the rest of the advanced world. Many other economies have grown at rates almost double that of the UK. This has been a cause of much public bewilderment and of a certain amount of despair, and in recent years the long-standing anxiety about slow growth has become overlaid with the more alarming fear that the UK economy cannot and will not grow at all. The post-war political and economic history of the UK is strewn with arguments about why this has happened and what can and should be done about it.

Since the mid-1960s there has been a steady stream of economic analyses of the causes of slow UK growth. The factors which economists have held to be crucial or important to the poor performance and prospects of the UK include limitations in the supply of labour available to the manufacturing sector, the poor performance of the manufacturing sector in international markets, the low share of investment in total output, the low rate of assimilation of technical progress, the excessive growth of spending in the non-market sector, the uncertainty generated by frequent and ill-advised changes in policy, and the increasing aggressiveness of organized labour. The mechanisms by which these factors have influenced growth have been variously presented as involving supply relationships, demand relationships, or some interaction between the two. As one would expect, recommended policies have been as varied as

1

the explanations offered. Despite the volume of this effort there has not emerged any substantial agreement amongst economists on causes and policy. Indeed the area of active controversy has increased in proportion to the volume of published work. Over the same period successive UK governments have come to power with the conviction that only a radically new strategy will improve economic growth. Labour administrations have decided that this requires greater State intervention in the economy, whereas Conservative Governments have held the opposite conviction, that greater reliance must be placed on the mechanisms of an enlarged and invigorated private sector. The present Conservative administration, unlike its Conservative and Labour predecessors, has not abandoned the radical strategy with which it came to power, and is determined to continue with its policies for the revitalization of the private sector. However, despite the efforts of economists and politicians the rate of UK economic growth has stubbornly remained less than that achieved elsewhere and during the 1970s has fallen to an average value barely greater than zero. Not surprisingly this outcome has encouraged the view that economics and economists have really nothing to say about the causes of growth, and that politicians are incapable of effective action.

I have tried to do four things in this book:

> (1) to set out the alternative hypotheses about the causes of growth which appear in the explanations offered by economists of why UK growth has been slower than that achieved in other advanced economies since the Second World War;
> (2) to see what support there is for these theoretical claims in the available evidence, including that presented by the authors of the claims;
> (3) to derive from (1) and (2) an explanation of slow UK growth, or at least an understanding of its immediate causes; and
> (4) to compare the growth strategy of the present Government with a policy which is consistent with this explanation.

Almost every explanation of UK growth reviewed in this

book is derived from the mainstream of economic theory; that is from neo-classical and Keynesian (or neo-Keynesian) theory. There are explanations of the post-war performance of the UK economy based on different traditions, for example Gamble and Walton (1976) and Purdy (1976), but in terms of insights actually offered they seem to me to add little to what conventional theory has to say. There is no logical reason to confine an assessment of policy to the present period. One can sensibly ask what could and should have been done in the past and what was the effect of what was actually done. The main reason for focusing on the present is that at the time of writing the UK economy is 1 year into a recession which is likely to make 3 million people unemployed and prove more severe than that of the worst years of the Great Depression. Options exist only in the present, and it is very important that those now available to the UK economy should be explored.

There are general difficulties involved in each of the four tasks set out above. The controversy over UK growth is not a disagreement about the strength of different relationships within a more-or-less agreed theoretical model of growth. The argument stems from very different views about the mechanisms of growth and how the economy as a whole works. Hypotheses pitched at this level are very difficult to test. For example, a key issue is whether or not an unregulated system of markets will generate steady economic expansion, but it is very difficult to put claims that it will or will not into a form susceptible to direct empirical test. There is almost no item of evidence on the UK economy which is wholly irrelevant to the question of slow growth, but much of what is available has not been assembled for the purpose of testing hypotheses about the causes of growth. It is thus possible to subject many claims only to indirect empirical tests involving the use of circumstantial evidence. This means that a fair amount of judgement has to be used in assessing the strength of claims about the causes of growth. The difficulty of formulating and testing claims about growth means that the empirical knowledge which can be drawn on for the formulation of policy is by no means complete.

Notwithstanding these problems, however, more can be

said about the causes of growth and policy than many commentators suppose. In particular I hope to show that by
using simple theory and empirical evidence it is possible to
identify the immediate causes of slow UK growth, to gain
some understanding of the underlying causes and mechanisms that have been at work, and, importantly, to say what
factors have not been significant. The reader who wishes to
start from a summary of conclusions on these issues should
look at the second section of chapter 7. It can also be shown
that an analysis of UK growth over the whole of the post-war
period provides a strong case against the growth strategy of
the present Conservative Government in favour of an alternative based on a policy of expansion. Although it is unlikely
that any reader will think otherwise, I should make it clear
from the outset that the alternative strategy advocated in the
discussion of policy is not original. A policy for growth
through expansion as an alternative to current policy has
been forcefully advocated by a number of writers including
Blake and Ormerod (1980), and most notably the members
of the Cambridge Economic Policy Group. The analysis in
this book does not lead to a hitherto undiscovered policy for
growth; but what I think can be claimed on the issue of
policy is that a comparative analysis of UK growth which
examines the effects over an extended period of a diverse set
of factors can make a useful contribution to the present
debate between the supporters of the Conservative strategy
and the advocates of the alternative of expansion.

The overall strategy I have adopted for the organization of
material is to examine first of all the question of which is the
key sector for economic growth. After that there is an
examination of a number of different claims about factors
which have constrained the expansion of this sector in the
UK. Most of the arguments presented by different investigators can be fitted into this framework without too much
difficulty. Finally there is an appraisal of current policies and
an argument in favour of the alternative of expansion. The
arrangement of material in chapters is as follows. Chapter 1
introduces what is to be explained and sets out a general
direction in which to proceed. In this chapter more space
than usual is devoted to the definition of economic growth.

This is because I believe that elements in the definition of what growth is can prejudice an inquiry into the causes of growth. Chapter 2 assesses the evidence for two rival arguments about which is the key sector for growth. In chapters 3, 4 and 5 the claims that the key sector in the UK has been supply constrained by labour, capital and productivity growth are set out together with the empirical evidence for and against. Chapter 6 draws together arguments about the importance of demand and examines the empirical support for the claim that UK growth has been retarded by a demand constraint imposed by poor trade performance. Some counter-arguments about the relationship between trade and growth are also examined here. Chapter 7 sets out what the conclusions of the previous chapters imply for the direction and components of a growth policy and argues that such a policy offers better prospects than that currently in force.

For reasons explained in chapter 1 the material in chapters 2–6 relates to the period 1950–73. Chapter 7 contains a section on UK growth in the period since 1973. In all chapters I have tried to present the material in such a way that only a limited prior knowledge of economic theory and statistical methods is required. The formal techniques that are employed are used to clarify arguments that are made elsewhere in words. I hope that everything in this book will be accessible to anyone who has taken a first-year university course in economics or its equivalent, and that a great deal of it will be comprehensible to anyone who has an active interest in the controversy about the performance of the UK economy.

Anyone who writes an assessment of the arguments of others is indebted to his or her sources. Almost without exception the works reviewed in this book have been written with a clarity which much reduces the problem of understanding and presenting the arguments contained in them. The reader should not rely alone on my exposition of the views of others, however, and should also read the original sources. Reading them is a pleasure. I should like to acknowledge three authors by name. I owe to the writings of Nicholas Kaldor my understanding of what I have called the 'trade-demand' hypothesis of growth and the importance for explanation and policy of the distinction between it and the neo-classical position. I have freely used his arguments, particularly in chapters 1, 2 and 6 in which the relevant sources are cited. 'Britain's Slow Industrial Growth: Increasing Inefficiency Versus Low Rate of Technical Change', by Stanislaw Gomulka, is a penetrating essay which helped me a great deal in working out a structure for chapter 5. Chapters 8 and 9 of *Balance of Payments Theory and the United Kingdom Experience*, by A. P. Thirwall, contain a comprehensive review of the evidence of UK trade performance which I found very helpful in the preparation of chapter 6. I should like to thank James Malcomson for advice on some fine points of growth theory, and I have been much helped by the typing and secretarial skills of Margaret Johnson. Any errors in this book are my responsibility.

GBS   University of York, June 1981

1 Facts and explanations

The starting point for any attempt to explain the comparative growth performance of the UK economy is an explicit statement of what is to be explained and a choice of the general direction in which the exercise is to proceed. Even such a limited task as this is not as straightforward as it might seem. The facts of economic growth are not self-evident. Estimates of the rate of economic growth have to be constructed and there are a number of alternative methods which can be used. Also it must be assumed in any explanation of the growth of different economies that the economic mechanisms through which causal factors (whatever they be) have produced different outcomes in different economies are more or less the same. Fortunately the requirement is not that general economic structures are identical but that they are sufficiently alike to allow the effects of specific causal factors to be isolated with reasonable accuracy. If this assumption cannot be made we are in the same position as someone trying to explain how a motor cycle can travel faster than a horse.

The record

The comparative growth record of the UK economy since the Second World War is well known and does not in itself require much elaboration. Over the period 1951–73 the annual rate of economic growth of the UK has been much less than that of the major industrial economies of Western Europe and of Canada and Japan, although closer to that of

7

Table 1.1
Annual rates of growth of GDP and GDP per man-hour at constant prices[1] (percentages)

	1870–1913		1922–1929		1929–1937		1951–1973	
	GDP	GDP/MH	GDP	GDP/MH	GDP	GDP/MH	GDP	GDP/MH
Belgium	2.0	1.2	3.4	1.6	0.1	0.1	4.1	4.5
Canada	3.8	2.0	6.2	1.2	-0.2	-1.7	5.1	3.1
Denmark	3.2	1.9	2.6	1.3	1.9	1.4	3.9	4.0
France	1.6	1.8	4.4	2.4	-0.5	1.0	5.1	4.9
Germany	2.8	1.9	4.2	0.7	2.6	2.3	5.9	5.8
Italy	1.5	1.2	2.9	1.8	1.4	2.7	5.2	5.3
Japan	2.5	1.8	2.9	1.2	4.8	1.6	9.5	7.5
Netherlands	1.9	1.2	3.5	2.4	0.2	-0.4	5.0	4.1
Norway	2.1	1.6	4.2	3.0	2.5	2.1	4.2	4.4
Sweden	2.8	2.4	5.0	1.2	2.2	2.4	3.8	3.8
UK	1.9	1.1	2.6	2.1	2.0	2.0	2.8	2.8
USA	4.1	2.1	3.3	2.7	-0.2	3.3	3.5	2.3

Source: Calculated from Maddison (1964, appendices G and H; 1977 and 1979).
[1]See note 1 on page 24.

the USA. The record of growth in output per man-hour is slightly more favourable showing a reduced spread and an improved ranking of the UK. Less well known is the post-war record of the UK in comparison to its achievements in earlier periods. The performance which has disappointed many has been by a small margin the best achieved over any comparable period over the last century; but for almost all other economies the post-war record has been very much better than that of earlier periods. The magnitudes involved are shown in table 1.1. Before looking at how these events might be explained it is important to say something about the definitions and measurements of economic growth which are presented in this table.

Definitions

The potential output (or productive potential) of an economy is determined by the volume of available factor inputs and the prevailing technology which governs their conversion into output. Potential output is the output that would be realized if labour and capital were fully employed and used at normal intensity. Economic growth is defined as the growth of the potential output of an economy over the long run. The rate of economic growth is the proportionate rate of growth of potential output. However this is not an operational definition because the rate of growth of observable and measurable output, that is the growth rate of actual output, may not equal the growth rate of potential output. The two rates will differ in an economy in which the overall pressure of demand varies through time but does not influence the growth of potential output. In this case the given growth rate of potential output will be exceeded by the growth rate of actual output if there is an increase in the pressure of demand from a situation in which spare capacity exists, and conversely will exceed the growth rate of actual output if the pressure of demand falls to create spare capacity. It follows directly from this that the growth rate of potential output in such an economy is the growth rate of actual output that would emerge under a constant pressure of demand. This is the operational definition of the rate of economic growth.

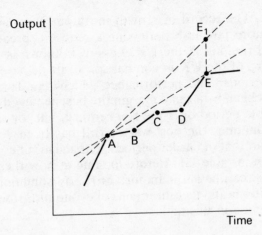

FIGURE 1.1   *The growth of output*

As there are some important distinctions involved in this definition it is worth amplifying this verbal statement with a simple diagram. In figure 1.1 time is measured horizontally and output measured vertically on a logarithmic scale. This arrangement has the convenient property that a constant proportionate growth rate appears as a straight line, and the steeper is the slope of the line the greater is the growth rate. ABCDE represents the path that output actually took under a varying pressure of demand. If the pressure of demand was equal at A and E and sufficient to maintain full employment we can say that the straight line AE represents the path that actual output would have taken had the pressure of demand been sustained at a full employment level. Thus AE represents the path of potential output and its slope represents the growth rate of output that conforms to the definition of economic growth. That the slope is positive indicates that the supply of factor inputs has increased and (or) that technical progress has occurred. The rate of economic growth thus defined is exceeded by the growth rate of actual output between B and C and exceeds the growth rate of actual output between C and D.

This definition of economic growth implies that the growth rate of potential output is independent of the pressure of demand. In figure 1.1 this means that changes in the pressure of demand do not result in changes in the slope of AE. If this were not the case it could no longer be said that the line AE represents the path that actual output would have taken under a higher (constant) pressure of demand than that which actually prevailed. If the growth of potential output is, say, a positive function of the pressure of demand, an increase in demand to a higher level than that achieved along ABCDE would have resulted in a rate of economic growth higher than that represented by the slope of AE and a level of potential output in the final period higher than that represented by E. In other words the line AE would have swung upwards from A to terminate at some point E_1 vertically above E. That the slope increases indicates that an increase in the pressure of demand induces an additional increase in the supply of factor inputs and (or) technical progress. In this case spare capacity would have existed (indicated by E being below E_1). In other words the line AE represents the path that actual output would have taken under a falling pressure of demand. The difficulty this result creates is that the rate of economic growth from A can now only be defined (and thus measured) in terms of an output level such as E_1 which was not actually achieved. This problem is avoided by the assumption that potential output is independent of the pressure of demand. It should be emphasized, however, that the status of this assumption in the definition of economic growth is not that of a claim about how an economy actually works but that of a device to allow a straightforward operational definition of the rate of economic growth.

Measurements

The simplest and most widely used technique for estimating economic growth is based directly on the definition presented above. A period is selected which separates two years (1 and N) in which the pressure of demand has been equal. The compound interest formula

$$Y_N = Y_1(1 + g_y)^{N-1}$$

provides an expression for the average percentage growth rate of Y

$$g_y = \left\{ \sqrt[N-1]{\frac{Y_N}{Y_1}} - 1 \right\} 100$$

which allows the growth rate to be estimated from data for the initial and final years. This is the method used to calculate the growth rates in table 1.1. Thus with the exception of the earliest period the terminal years of each period for each country have been of a roughly equivalent high pressure of demand as indicated by low unemployment rates. This is a rough and ready method. The pressure of demand may not in fact have been equal in the selected terminal years with the result that the growth rate is miscalculated. An estimate of the growth rate which is much less sensitive to the choice of terminal years can be derived from regression analysis[2] used to fit an exponential growth curve of the form $Y = ab^t$. However for this study there is not a great deal at stake in the choice between these alternatives because the use of one method rather than another does not give a different picture of the growth performance of the UK relative to the achievements of other economies.

Since 1973 all advanced economies have experienced a prolonged recession in which average growth rates have been at or just below one-half of the level of the period from 1951 to 1973. It is not easy to say whether this experience represents a major cyclical slump which will eventually correct itself or be corrected, or a clear structural break in the momentum of post-war growth and thus the emergence of a new trend of slower growth for all economies. For this reason the period since 1973 is examined briefly by itself in the third section of chapter 7. This positioning also helps to set the scene for the discussion of current policy which takes up the remaining part of that chapter. Chapters 2–6 are concerned with the UK growth performance in the two decades before 1973.

Explanations

Academic and popular debate has thrown up many different views on the causes of the slow growth of the UK economy since the war. The chapters which follow are restricted to an assessment of those explanations which are (1) logically sound and (2) susceptible to some form of measurement and empirical testing. The difficulty with arguments which stress the importance of qualitative factors alone is that they are very difficult if not impossible to resolve; also they do not allow for an assessment of the relative importance of different factors. Quantitative hypotheses allow more to be said. Of course it does not follow from this that factors which are not quantifiable have been unimportant. Qualitative hypotheses may be correct and quantitative hypotheses may end up saying very little. This possibility is the potential cost of imposing condition (2). On these two conditions a number of would-be explanations can be excluded from the inquiry at the outset. We can also reject several admissible explanations which do not seem to be borne out by the available evidence.

Some rejected explanations

Illogical explanations usually involve a confusion either (1) between the growth of output and the level of output or (2) over the relevant standard of comparison. It is usually possible to recast such explanations in a logical form but the resulting explanations are often implausible. An example of (1) is the popular argument that the poor growth record of the UK has been the result of relative inefficiency in the form of overmanning (more man-hours per machine) and underproduction (less output from each machine). The direct effect of such inefficiency would be a level of labour productivity and output lower than that of a more efficient system. The condition of a lower growth rate of output and productivity is increasing relative inefficiency. Thus the logically sound form of the argument is that the UK has suffered from a faster increase in overmanning and underproduction than other economies. This is not the form in which the argument is normally put. Of course it is possible that the level of efficiency may influence the rate of growth through a much less direct mechanism involving, say, a relationship between the extent of restrictive practices and the rate of technical innovation. Such links are invariably not specified. An exception is the argument of Kilpatrick and Lawson (1980) that the industrial decline of the UK is partly attributable to the depressing effects on productivity growth of a decentralized structure of collective bargaining. This view is briefly examined in chapter 5. An example of (2) is the equally popular idea that poor performance has been a result of errors in government policy. It may be that the UK growth rate has been lower than it could have been under different policies; but it could have only been lower than those of other economies for this reason if more errors or more damaging errors had been committed in the UK than elsewhere. The correction makes the argument rather implausible.

The most widely canvassed qualitative hypothesis stresses what is variously described as 'the social climate' or the 'national character'. The gist of this position seems to be that economic performance depends at least in part on social reward and that British society has been unique in the extent to which it has deprecated commercial and technological skills. The most recent expression of this view appears in the report of the Finniston Committee which attributes poor economic performance in the UK to an insufficient use of engineering skills. Thus

> great prestige is attached to science, medicine and the creative arts . . . but there is no cultural equivalent in Britain, and hence no basis for according similar esteem, to the European concepts conveyed in German by 'technik'–the synthesis of knowledge from many different disciplines to devise technical and economic solutions to practical problems (Cmnd 7794, 1980, p. 25).

The difficulty here is one of evidence. As will be clear in the following chapters there is no explanation of UK growth for which the recording and interpretation of evidence is easy, but the additional problem in this case is in knowing what it is that should be recorded in the first place. What class of events in the world (apart of course from measured growth rates) could bear out assertions about the degrees of social esteem attached to different skills in different countries? If the form of reliable evidence cannot be specified it is difficult to see how the argument could be settled.

The 'catching-up' and 'stop–go' hypotheses are explanations which seem to be incorrect. It could be argued from table 1.1 that the superior performance of most other economies since 1951 has been no more than a compensating response to the slump of the 1930s in which the deviation from the trends of the period before 1930 was greater in most other economies than in the UK. Alternatively this explanation can be advanced one period to argue that the post-war experience represents a readjustment to pre-1938 trends which were disturbed by the Second World War to a greater degree in continental Europe than in the UK (and Canada and the USA). The advocates of this view are not usually explicit about how this self-righting mechanism works, but this difficulty apart the argument does not stand up well to empirical scrutiny. Beckerman (1965, ch. 1) has shown that the growth performance of Germany, Canada and the USA from 1950 to 1960 is consistent with the second formulation but that for seven other European economies including the UK there is no significant correlation between growth rates over this period and deviations from trend in 1950. Both formulations are inconsistent with estimates of productivity growth over the longer period to 1976 provided by Maddison (1979). Growth rates of output per man-hour from 1950 to 1976 in France, Germany, Italy and Japan (the fastest-growing economies) have been substantially greater than those that would have been required to restore pre-war trends over this period. Under prevailing policies the mechanisms of the UK economy of the 1950s and 1960s generated moderate cyclical fluctuations in employment inflation and the balance of payments. The 'stop–go' hypothesis is that the uncertainties generated by this experience have undermined investment, innovation and thus ultimately growth. Again there seems to be no empirical support for this view. Whiting's (1976) evidence on seven major OECD economies is that over the period

1955–73 the UK has, in terms of net manufacturing output, experienced the smallest percentage deviation from trend growth and the lowest rate of trend growth, whereas the two fastest-growing economies (Italy and Japan) showed the greatest levels of instability. The results are consistent with Wilson's earlier (1969) finding that over the period 1950–65 stability and growth rates in 13 advanced economies were not positively correlated.

The supply of resources

The area which remains after these exclusions is still very large indeed. Most empirical investigations of comparative growth rates have started implicitly or explicitly from the assumption that the supply of resources is exogenous. We have seen that the assumption that the growth of resources and potential output is independent of the pressure of demand is a part of the definition of economic growth; but terms accepted within a definition should not be confused with or taken for a true statement about how the world works. It may or may not be the case that the supply of resources is in fact independent of demand. The assumption that this is the case implies that the factors determining the growth of resources lie outside the system of output growth being analysed. The boundaries of the analysis are thus drawn in such a way as to identify the growth of resources as the cause of economic growth. This means that for an explanation of the growth of an economy relative to another we should look no further than the growth of resources in each system.

Provided that capital and labour are substitutable and that increases in capital, labour and productivity are independent, the relationship between the growth of resources and output in an economy can be expressed as

$$g_y = \alpha g_k + \beta g_l + \lambda, \qquad (1.1)$$

where g_y, g_k, g_l and λ are respectively the growth rates of output, capital, labour and output per unit of total input (which is merely the residual between g_y and αg_k plus βg_l), and where α and β are measures of the responsiveness of output growth to capital and labour growth (partial elasticities of output with respect to capital and labour). It follows from the assumption that g_k, g_l and λ are exogenous that differences in national growth rates derive from differences in the contributions from capital, labour and productivity growth; but to say this is not to say very much. More precise statements about the nature and relative importance of the components of capacity growth cannot be made without additional assumptions of which the number of plausible alternatives is large.

If it is assumed that the underlying production function exhibits constant returns to scale, that factor markets are perfectly competitive, that productivity growth is exogenous and augments both factors (i.e. is neutral) and augments old and new factors alike (i.e. is disembodied), then α and β sum to 1 and are equal to relative factor shares, and λ is due solely to the growth of knowledge. These results are derived in an appendix to this chapter. But if the exogenously given rate of technical progress λ comes through improvements in the skills of all members of the labour force the growth equation becomes

$$g_y = \alpha g_k + \beta(g_l + \lambda). \tag{1.2}$$

The contribution of technical progress to output growth falls absolutely and relatively as it now must operate through the labour elasticity which by previous assumption is less than 1. An analogous conclusion holds for autonomous technical progress which is capital augmenting. An alternative assumption which is very plausible is that technical progress comes only through improvements in the efficiency of new machines. A simple model of capital embodied autonomous technical progress at the rate λ yields the growth equation

$$g_y = \alpha(1+\bar{a}\lambda)g_k + \beta g_l + \alpha\lambda, \tag{1.3}$$

where $\bar{a}$ is the average age of machines.[3] The new result in this case is that the sensitivity of output growth to capital accumulation is increase in absolute and relative terms because investment now provides both more machines and newer and therefore more efficient machines. Yet another formulation emerges if the assumption that technical progress is exogenous is relaxed. One of the best-known descriptions of endogenous technical progress is provided by Arrow's model of learning-by-doing in which improvements in output per worker (labour augmenting technical progress) are not exogenous but depend upon work experience. A proxy for experience is the cumulative past investment of the economy which is the same thing as the current capital stock if capital does not depreciate. This relationship can be expressed as

$$\lambda = g_k \cdot m$$

which says that the growth rate of output per worker equals the growth rate of the capital stock (the index of experience) times the elasticity of output per worker with respect to capital (m) which reflects the rate of learning from experience and is assumed to be less than 1. This expression can be substituted into equation (1.2) to give

$$g_y = \alpha g_k + \beta(g_l + g_k \cdot m), \qquad (1.4)$$

which can be rewritten as

$$g_y = g_k(\alpha + \beta m) + \beta g_l. \qquad (1.5)$$

Capital accumulation now stimulates technical progress through the learning process and thus makes an additional indirect contribution to output growth.[4] This result is very like that of equation (1.1) without technical progress but with increasing returns to scale the condition of which is that the sum of the coefficients on g_k and g_l is greater than 1. The only difference between the two cases is that the effects of learning through experience are irreversible and thus, unlike the effects of increasing returns to scale, cannot be lost by any subsequent reduction in the scale of activity.

These equations provide a set of alternative frameworks within which observed differences in national growth rates can be attributed to differences in the contributions from the right-hand side variables. The problem of course is in knowing which permutation of assumptions about market structures, the technology of production and technical progress is correct. The assumptions most often used are of perfect competition, constant returns to scale and exogenous technical progress. However, they are chosen not for their accuracy but because they allow the use of relatively simple computational procedures. The most famous study of comparative growth rates based on these assumptions is that of Denison (1967 and 1968) which is examined in chapter 3.

These difficulties apart, there are two respects in which any of the above hypotheses must be modified. The first concerns the effect of demand factors on growth. The second is about dis-aggregation and thus concerns the effect on the overall growth rate of the balance of activity between sectors of economies.

Demand and resources

In the long run it is impossible for an economy to grow at a faster rate than that allowed by the growth of resources. Actual output cannot grow faster than potential output; but the growth of resources may not in fact be independent of the growth of demand and thus of the actual performance of the system in terms of the growth of output and income actually achieved. The issue here is often expressed as whether growth is demand induced or supply constrained. This is rather misleading because long-run growth is always supply constrained. The real issue is the extent to which the supply of resources and thus potential output is demand induced or exogenously given.

There are several mechanisms by which the growth of potential output may be influenced by the growth of actual output and thus demand. The most obvious possible link is between output growth and capital accumulation. Thus in Kaldor's view

> savings and capital accumulation in a capitalist economy do not represent an independent variable—a faster rate of growth induces a higher rate of investment; it also brings about a higher share of savings to finance that investment, through its effect on the share of profits (Kaldor, 1968, p. 390).

This effect of actual output on potential output will be reinforced if technical progress is embodied in new capital
equipment. Alternatively if technical progress emerges
through a learning process potential output will expand as a
result of the experience provided by the growth of actual
output or capital. A faster growth of demand may also
increase the effective supply of labour and capital through
immigration from other economies and through the reallocation of factors from low-productivity to high-productivity
occupations.

To see the effect that an allowance for demand factors can
have on the analysis outlined in the previous section consider the simplest form of the accelerator mechanism.
Assume that output (Y) and the capital stock (K) can be
expressed as continuous functions of time (t). Let the desired
capital stock be a constant proportion of the level of output,
and assume that the actual capital stock is instantaneously
adjusted to the desired capital stock through investment.
Thus

$$K = vY \qquad (1.6)$$

where v is the accelerator coefficient (the constant average
and marginal capital output ratio). Investment (the change
in the capital stock) will therefore be a constant proportion
of the change in output

$$I = \frac{dK}{dt} = \frac{vdY}{dt} \qquad (1.7)$$

It follows from (1.6) that output and capital will grow at the
same rate, that is $g_y = g_k$. Now go back to equation (1.1). If
g_l and λ are maintained in the long run there will emerge
direct and indirect effects on g_y. The direct effects will be βg_l
and λ. The indirect effects will work through the accelerator
mechanism. Thus in the case of the growth of the labour
force, a growth of output of βg_l will induce a growth of
capital of βg_l via the accelerator which will generate an additional growth of output of $\alpha\beta g_l$ which will induce a further
growth of capital of $\alpha\beta g_l$, and so on. Technical progress at

the rate λ will have similar effects. βg_l and λ can be thought of as the short-run contributions which emerge in the period before interactions between g_y and g_k begin. The total direct and indirect effects of g_l and λ can be seen by substituting g_y for g_k in (1.1). Thus

$$g_y = \alpha g_y + \beta g_l + \lambda$$

$$g_y = \frac{\beta g_l}{1 - \alpha} + \frac{\lambda}{1 - \alpha} \qquad (1.8)$$

The dependence of g_k on g_y has the effects of (1) multiplying the direct contributions of labour force growth and technical progress by $1/(1 - \alpha)$ and (2) eliminating capital accumulation as an independent source or cause of growth. Of course (2) does not imply that the relationship between K and Y described by the production function is irrelevant to the growth of output, for the greater is the output–capital elasticity the more powerful is the growth multiplier.

If it is also the case that all other components of demand are endogenous (together with the supply of labour and technical progress), we end up with the unhelpful conclusion that everything depends upon everything else. For this reason the demand model attaches special importance to those components of demand which come nearest to being independent of the growth of output and income in the system being analysed. Exports from the system are usually thought of as the key component on the assumption that the other components besides investment are more nearly endogenous; specifically that private consumption and public expenditure depend on personal income and tax revenues whereas exports are financed by income growth in other economies. It is not implausible to expect that demand effects on growth will be self-reinforcing. An improvement in productivity induced by external demand which results in improved competitiveness may attract additional demand in foreign and domestic markets which will give a further boost to productivity and so on. Thus although external demand must be relied on to initiate growth, other components may contribute to the propagation process which follows.

Demand effects which spread in a cumulative way have an obvious attraction as explanations of divergent international trends in growth which persist over the long run.

If demand effects are very strong the view of output growth presented in the previous section is more or less completely overturned. Thus 'in the long run there is no such thing as an exogenously given output potential; it all depends on the path actually followed as determined by the success of the economy in attracting external demand for its products' (Kaldor, 1980). The boundaries of the analysis are thus entirely redrawn so as to identify the growth in external demand as the cause of economic growth. This implies that differences between the growth rates of economies are to be explained by differences in demand conditions of which differences in the supply of resources are merely a reflection. This conclusion amounts to a denial of Say's Law and can thus be objected to on general theoretical grounds. Since economic activity consists of the exchange of commodities against commodities, an increase in resources and the supply of commodities creates the demand for other commodities. It can therefore be argued that it makes no economic sense to say that the expansion of output is constrained by demand. The effective constraint must ultimately be the supply of resources. The general reply to this point is that demand is an effective constraint if conditions required for the operation of Say's Law do not in fact obtain. This issue is examined in chapter 6 in which the demand model is set out in more detail.

Before passing on it should be noted that for some of its advocates the demand hypothesis expresses both a distinctive view on the causes of growth and a much more general objection to orthodox economic analysis. The underlying claim of the demand model as presented, for example, by Kaldor (1975a) is that the function of markets is to organize a cumulative expansion of output through the creation of more resources, and not, as the neo-classical theory of market supposes, to secure an equilibrium in which a given quantum of resources is optimally allocated in the light of output gained and foregone. The general objection is thus that a neo-classical analysis of markets based on the concepts of 'equilibrium' and 'opportunity cost' is a misrepresentation of how advanced market economies actually work.

Dualism demand and resources

A feature of most serious studies of UK growth has been the disaggregation of overall activity into sectors. The underlying view has been that all sectors are not equally important for economic growth; specifically that there is an economic relationship between overall growth performance and the performance of one sector which is much weaker or non-existent in other sectors. The message of this approach is that growth depends on the balance of activity between sectors. However investigators do not agree on the criterion for disaggregation. UK growth has been analysed by Kaldor (1966) in terms of a dichotomy between manufacturing and non-manufacturing sectors and by Bacon and Eltis (1978) in terms of a division between market and non-market sectors.

The implication of dual models of this kind is that an explanation of differences in national growth rates is to be found in the factors which have governed the expansion of the key sector in different economies. There are two quite distinct questions involved in this approach. First, can economic growth in an advanced economy be causally related to the growth of a key sector? Secondly, if it can, why has the expansion of this sector (and thus overall growth) been slower in the UK than elsewhere? The first question is dealt with in the next chapter in the form of an assessment of the alternative proposals of Kaldor, and Bacon and Eltis. The second issue can be investigated by applying to the sectoral economy the supply and demand analysis outlined in the previous two sections at the level of the economy as a whole. The specific question here is thus whether the slow expansion of the key sector in the UK is to be explained by a slow growth of demand for its output or by a slow growth of resources which did not depend upon the expansion actually achieved. This issue is much more complicated than the first and is examined in chapters 3, 4, 5 and 6. It is however a key issue for policy, for a conclusion one way or the other makes a great deal of difference to what it would be sensible for a government to do if it wishes to see an improvement in growth.

Notes

1. The terminal years for individual countries are as in table 1.1 except for:

Belgium	1923–28, 1928–37
Canada	1923–28, 1928–37
Denmark	1923–30, 1930–37, 1950–73
Germany	1922–28, 1928–37
Italy	1923–28, 1928–37, 1951–74
Netherlands	1922–30, 1930–37
Norway	1922–30, 1930–37
Sweden	1923–29, 1929–37, 1951–74
U.K.	1924–29, 1929–37
U.S.	1923–29, 1929–37

2. See Floud (1979, ch. 4 section d, and ch. 6) for a very clear introduction to semi-logarithmic graphs and the definition and measurement of growth rates.
3. See Branson and Litvack (1976, pp. 391–4) for a demonstration of this result.
4. See Haache (1979, ch. 9.2) for a demonstration of this result. It should be noted that in this case α and β will not equal relative factor shares unless endogenous technical progress takes the form of an external economy. For a demonstration of this see Haache (1979, p. 145).

Appendix: The production function and the growth equation

A production function which satisfies the conditions of constant returns to scale and exogenous, neutral and disembodied productivity growth is the Cobb–Douglas form

$$Y = AK^{\alpha}L^{\beta} \qquad \alpha + \beta = 1 \qquad (1.9)$$

where Y is output, A is an index of total factor productivity, K is an index of the capital stock and L is an index of the labour input. Constant returns to scale obtains when the result of multiplying K and L by a constant, say f, is to multiply output by the same constant. Thus

$$A(fK)^\alpha (fL)^\beta$$
$$= f^{\alpha+\beta} A K^\alpha L^\beta \quad (1.10)$$

which, as $\alpha + \beta = 1$, equals $fAK^\alpha L^\beta$ which equals fY.

Taking natural logarithms of (1.9) and differentiating throughout with respect to time gives

$$\frac{d}{dt}(\ln Y) = \frac{d}{dt}(\ln A) + \frac{\alpha d}{dt}(\ln K) + \frac{\beta d}{dt}(\ln L) \quad (1.11)$$

The rule

$$\frac{d}{dt}(\ln x) = \frac{dx}{dt}\frac{1}{x} \text{ for the function } x = f(t)$$

allows (1.11) to be written as

$$g_y = \alpha g_k + \beta g_l + \lambda \quad (1.12)$$

where g_y, g_k, g_l, and λ are respectively the growth rates of output, capital, labour, and total productivity, and where α and β are the partial elasticities of output with respect to capital and labour.

Profit-maximizing behaviour in perfectly competitive markets will ensure that the rate of real reward to capital and labour will equal the marginal physical product of capital and labour respectively. Marginal physical products are obtained by differentiating (1.9) with respect to K and L. Thus

$$\frac{\partial Y}{\partial K} = A\alpha K^{\alpha-1} L^\beta$$

$$= \frac{\alpha A K^\alpha L^\beta}{K}$$

$$= \frac{\alpha Y}{K} \quad (1.13)$$

$$\frac{\partial Y}{\partial L} = A K^\alpha \beta L^{\beta-1}$$

$$= \frac{\beta A K^{\alpha} L^{\beta}}{L}$$

$$= \frac{\beta Y}{L}. \tag{1.14}$$

The total real payment to each factor is the rate of reward times the number of units employed. Thus

$$Y_k = \frac{\alpha Y K}{K}$$

$$= \alpha Y \tag{1.15}$$

$$\therefore \frac{Y_k}{Y} = \alpha \tag{1.16}$$

$$Y_l = \frac{\beta Y L}{L}$$

$$= \beta Y \tag{1.17}$$

$$\therefore \frac{Y_l}{Y} = \beta. \tag{1.18}$$

(1.16) and (1.18) show that under the specified conditions relative factors shares are equal to output elasticities.

2 The key sector in economic growth

The belief that economic growth depends on the expansion of a key sector was formalized in the eighteenth century Physiocratic analysis of the production and distribution of agricultural output and has persisted in various forms ever since. Before we examine the details of the relevant modern formulations it is worth considering a general objection to the key sector hypothesis. It may be argued that changes in the relative size of sectors are a normal feature of growth in advanced economies. For example, if the income elasticity of demand for the output of a sector is greater than 1 the share of the sector in total output will rise as growth proceeds. Alternatively, a sector in an open economy may expand relative to others as a result of growing international specialization. In either case the relative expansion of a sector is no more than an adjustment to changing market conditions which are a part of the process of growth. The basic claim of the 'market adjustment' argument is thus that changes in the balance between sectors are a consequence or byproduct of growth and expansion and not a cause of it. Several variants of this argument involving trade adjustments are examined in chapter 6. All that needs to be said at this point is that the argument would interpret a positive relationship between the relative size of a sector and overall growth as showing the effect of growth on the balance of sectors and not the reverse. That reverse causal relationships do in fact exist is the message which is common to the very different arguments of Kaldor, and Bacon and Eltis. Thus it is to these arguments that we can turn for one evaluation of the 'market adjustment' view.

The manufacturing sector as the engine of growth

The key role assigned to the manufacturing sector has been a central element of Kaldor's analysis (1966, 1975b) of the comparative growth performance of the UK. Other investigators taking the same view include Tarling and Cripps (1973), Cornwall (1977a, ch. VII and ch. VII section E) and Singh (1977). The argument starts with the evidence that within the group of advanced economies faster overall growth has been positively associated with the share of manufacturing activity. The striking feature of table 2.1 is that from 1950 to 1973 the fastest-growing economies, in particular Italy, Japan and Germany, experienced the largest increase in the share of manufacturing output in total output. A precise expression of this association is provided by a regression of the growth rate of GDP (q) on the growth rate of manufacturing output (q_m).

$$q = 1.295 + 0.603q_m \qquad R^2 = 0.899 \qquad (2.1)$$
$$(0.031)$$

Source: Cripps and Tarling (1973), 12 advanced countries 1950–70, standard error in parentheses.

In no other sector apart from commerce is the correlation

Table 2.1
Manufacturing output as a proportion of GDP at 1963 prices, 1950–73

	1950	1960	1973
UK	29.3	31.0	31.5
Belgium	—	26.0	31.7
France	32.6	35.0	39.6
Germany	31.0	39.9	44.6
Italy	17.9	25.5	32.0
Netherlands	32.7	36.6	42.3
Canada	25.1	24.2	27.1
Japan	—	31.7	41.8
Sweden	25.2	27.7	32.5
USA	28.2	27.4	29.2

Source: Brown and Sheriff (1979).

between output growth and GDP growth as close. These regression results are a confirmation of earlier results obtained by Kaldor (1966) and United Nations (1970). It can easily be calculated from equation (2.1) that growth rates of output above about $3\frac{1}{4}$ per cent are associated with a growth rate of manufacturing output greater than the growth rate of total output–that is with the share of manufacturing output rising and the share of all other sectors falling. That a correlation exists between q and q_m is not surprising since manufacturing output is a large component of total output. However equation (2.1) does not depend on double-counting since the relationship is not significantly disturbed by the exclusion of manufacturing output from the left-hand side.

A similar relationship holds between the growth rate of GDP and the relative growth of manufacturing employment. The data for Italy, Germany and Japan in table 2.2 again suggest a positive relationship between output growth and the employment share in manufacturing. Kaldor (1968) has shown the existence of a strong statistical relationship between rates of growth of GDP and the growth rates of manufacturing employment in 12 advanced countries for the period 1953/4–1963/4, and the lack of any relationship between GDP growth rates and rates of growth of total employment over the same period.

Table 2.2
Proportions of total employment in manufacturing, 1950–73

	1950	1960	1973
UK	34.7	35.8	32.3
Belgium	32.7	33.5	31.8
France	—	27.9	27.9
Germany	—	34.7	36.1
Italy	—	26.6	32.2
Netherlands	30.2	28.6	24.7
Japan	—	21.3	27.4
Sweden	—	32.1	27.5
USA	34.4	33.6	31.6

Source: Brown and Sheriff (1979).

These results have not been questioned by other investigators, but of course the amount of disputable information they contain is very small. They are correctly regarded by their producers as statements of empirical regularities in need of an economic explanation. Much more controversial are the specific explanations that have been advanced to account for these observations. Most explanations seem to rest on at least one of the following points: that manufacturing (1) has been able to employ resources at low opportunity cost, (2) has by its expansion generated growth in other sectors and (3) has been a source of technical progress and in particular of dynamic economies of scale. Of course the position on all points must be that these features are non-existent or at least much less significant in other sectors. The first point is essentially that

> it could . . . be true that the growth of industrial output was the governing factor in the overall rate of economic growth so long as the growth of industrial output represented a net addition to the use of resources and not just a transfer of resources from one use to another. This would be the case if (a) the capital required for industrial production was (largely or wholly) self-generated . . . and (b) the labour engaged in industry had no true opportunity cost outside industry on account of the prevalence of disguised unemployment in agriculture and services (Kaldor, 1975b, pp. 894 and 895).

The second point is

> that the manufacturing sector takes on importance as the sector propelling the rest of the economy not only because of the large number of backward linkages in the traditional input–output sense. In addition, important sub-sectors of manufacturing have been the main purveyors of technological and technical progress throughout much of the rest of the economy (Cornwall, 1977a, p. 135).

It is fair to say that both of these points are presented as plausible assumptions rather than empirically supported conclusions. They have not been subject to systematic empirical testing and are therefore best regarded as unproven. There is however much more evidence on the hypothesis of dynamic economies of scale in manufacturing.

A positive and reversible relationship between the level of productivity and the scale of production is usually termed increasing returns to scale and is thought to depend on factors such as indivisibilities and the division of labour under a given state of technology. In contrast dynamic economies of scale are shown in a relationship between the growth rate of productivity and the growth rate of production which derives from general improvements in technical knowledge and specific innovations induced by the experience provided by output growth. Dynamic economies of scale are thus a form of endogenous technical progress which is indistinguishable from the example of learning-by-doing presented in the previous chapter. The general argument is that as this form of technical progress is more or less exclusive to the manufacturing sector the overall growth rate of productivity and therefore output will be greater the greater is the growth of manufacturing output.

The identity

$$g_m \equiv g_{pm} + g_{em},$$

where g_m is the growth rate of manufacturing output, g_{pm} is the growth rate of labour productivity in manufacturing and g_{em} is the growth rate of employment in manufacturing, allows the concept of dynamic economies of scale to be expressed in two different ways. Thus

$$g_{pm} = a + bg_m \tag{2.2}$$

$$g_{em} = -a + (1 - b)g_m \tag{2.3}$$

are two different ways of looking at the same positive linear relationship between productivity growth and output growth in manufacturing. Of course if g_{em} is constant (k) or zero the correlation between g_{pm} and g_m will be perfect since g_{pm} will equal g_m minus k by definition. Thus the condition for the existence of a meaningful economic relationship is that b is positive but significantly less than 1. This relationship was first investigated by Verdoorn (1949). Kaldor's (1966) results for 12 advanced economies for the period 1953/4–1963/4 are

$$g_{pm} = \quad 1.035 + 0.484 g_m \qquad R^2 = 0.826 \qquad (2.4)$$
$$(0.070)$$

$$g_{em} = -1.028 + 0.516 g_m \qquad R^2 = 0.844 \qquad (2.5)$$
$$(0.070)$$

with standard errors in parentheses. The interpretation of these results is that when g_m is zero manufacturing productivity increases at a rate of just over 1 per cent (and therefore labour requirements fall at a rate of just over 1 per cent) on account of exogenous technical progress. Each percentage addition to the growth of manufacturing output induces a growth of productivity through dynamic economies of scale of just under one-half of 1 per cent and thus requires an increase in employment of just over one-half of 1 per cent. These results have been confirmed by more recent investigations by Vaciago (1975) for 1950–69 and by Cornwall (1977a, ch. VII) for 1950–70. Kaldor discovered positive but weaker relationships between productivity growth and output growth in construction and public utilities whereas in agriculture, mining, and transport and communications the autonomous component was much more important.

An objection to these results is that the influence of output growth on productivity growth is exaggerated by the omission of a measure of investment performance which would reveal the effect on productivity growth of the introduction of more and better machinery. The inclusion of the gross investment output ratio as an independent variable in equation (2.4) does decrease the coefficient on output growth from about one-half to one-quarter but does not render it statistically insignificant and therefore does not eliminate the positive association between productivity growth and output growth. This finding relates to the industrial sector – that is manufacturing plus construction and public utilities – and is in Kaldor (1967, appendix C). However it is not clear that the gross investment ratio is the most appropriate measure of investment performance in this context. One would expect the growth rate of output per worker to depend more on the growth rate of capital per worker than on the ratio of investment to output in the sector.

The two major objections to Kaldor's results have been

(1) that regressions of g_{pm} and g_{em} on g_m are an incorrect test of dynamic economies of scale and that the application of a correctly specified test provides no evidence of dynamic economies of scale; and

(2) that in any case the association between g_{pm} and g_m reflects the impact of technical progress on output growth rather than the reverse.

A requirement of the regression analysis which provides the results in (2.4) and (2.5) is that the right-hand side variable be exogenous to the system under scrutiny. Rowthorn's argument (1975b) is that over much of the post-war period output has been regulated by demand-management policies designed to ensure the employment of a growing labour force. Thus g_{em} and not g_m should be used as the independent variable in the regression analysis. Equation (2.2) should be rewritten as

$$g_{pm} = c + dg_{em} \qquad (2.6)$$

alternatively using the definition

$$g_m = c + (1 + d)g_{em}. \qquad (2.7)$$

Kaldor's response (1975b) is that owing to the existence of reserves of unemployed or underemployed labour in agriculture and services manufacturing employment has adjusted passively to changes in output induced by changes in exogenous components of demand, particularly exports. Thus g_m and not g_{em} should be regarded as exogenous. A good deal seems to hinge on which position is adopted. The positive relationship between g_{pm} and g_{em} discovered by Cripps and Tarling (1973) in 12 countries obtains only for a particular period – 1950–65 – and then only if the single untypical observation for Japan is included in the sample.[1] On the other hand a strong positive relationship exists be-

tween g_{pm} and g_m for 18 countries over the whole period
1950–69[2] and the exclusion of Japan does not seriously disturb the relationship between g_{pm}, g_{em} and g_m shown in (2.4)
and (2.5). It seems unlikely that this issue can be fully settled
by the techniques adopted by the protagonists. In the long
run there is likely to be a simultaneous interaction between
the supply of labour and the demand for output operating
through both of the mechanisms referred to by Kaldor and
Rowthorn. In these circumstances statistical estimates of the
parameters of any single equation will be subject to simultaneous equation bias and thus provide misleading conclusions about the relationships at work. The only investigation
to make provision for this that of Parikh (1978) in which the
possibility of an interaction between g_{em} and g_m is allowed for
and appropriate estimating techniques are used. For 12
advanced economies for the period 1950–70 the results are
that the influence of g_{em} on g_m has been insignificant and that
g_{em} has been determined by g_m which in turn has been determined by the growth of exports. It thus seems correct to
regard manufacturing output as the exogenous variable and
to reject the first objection to Kaldor's demonstration of
dynamic economies of scale in manufacturing. However,
even if it were valid this objection would merely establish
that one particular explanation of the observed relationship
between overall growth and manufacturing activity is incorrect. The second objection is potentially much more damaging to the hypothesis that manufacturing is the engine of
growth, for it amounts to the assertion that manufacturing
expansion is a consequence or byproduct of economic
growth and not a cause of it.

The argument in simple terms is that differential growth
rates of productivity have not been generated endogenously
within the manufacturing sectors of advanced economies but
have arisen exogenously amongst them to generate differential growth rates of output through effects on relative costs,
prices and thus demand in both domestic and foreign markets. This claim of course is an expression of the 'market
adjustment' argument introduced in the opening section of
this chapter. Advocates of this position such as Rowthorn
(1975b) are under an obligation to provide an explanation

of why technical progress has not been equally available to all. How this might have come about is examined in chapter 5. This apart, if it is to serve as an explanation of the observations described in equation (2.4) this argument must commit itself to two specific assumptions:

(1) that differential movements in productivity amongst advanced economies have been reflected in relative price movements rather than in relative wage movements; and

(2) that price elasticities of demand for manufacturing output in international markets have been such as to generate the observed movements in manufacturing output.

If (1) were correct price movements would be proportional to productivity movements and the implied, required, price elasticity for any economy would be approximately equal to its average growth rate of manufacturing output divided by its average growth rate of manufacturing productivity. Kaldor's (1966, p. 14) data for 12 countries for the period 1953/4–1963/4 shows that for no country is this figure less than 1 and for most it is between $1\frac{1}{2}$ and 2. However these figures are underestimates since the movement in the relative price of the manufacturing output of an economy will be less than the movement in manufacturing productivity in the economy if the growth of manufacturing productivity is positive in other economies. Evidence cited by Kennedy (1971, pp. 179 and 180) suggests that relative price changes have been less than proportional to productivity changes, which means that still higher price elasticities must be assumed. Unfortunately the available evidence on international price elasticities is not in the precise form required to test any such assumption since separate estimates of price elasticities for imports and exports do not measure the responsiveness of demand to relative price changes in both domestic and foreign markets. Thus a conclusive answer on this question is not possible. However the evidence on import and export price elasticities[3] does not suggest that the relevant elasticities have been high enough to explain the observed relationship between productivity and output growth in manufacturing. If this conclusion is correct it does not of course rule out the possibility that exogenous productivity growth has had some effect on output growth. It seems unlikely, however, that such effects can explain more than a small part of the observed relationship between output growth and productivity growth in manufacturing.

The conclusion these arguments point to is that Kaldor's hypothesis that manufacturing is the key growth sector stands up reasonably well to the specific objections that have been raised against it. However, the fact that there is some support for the hypothesis does not mean that for the purpose of analysing growth the dichotomy between manufacturing and non-manufacturing is superior to other schemes of disaggregation.

The market sector as the engine of growth

In a provocative study which has attracted much public and political attention Bacon and Eltis (1978) provide an analysis of Britain's post-war economic performance grounded on the view that 'all economies have a sector which produces a surplus off which the rest of the economy lives . . . the surplus creating sector of economies is the market sector' (Eltis, 1979a, p. 118). Although the author's main concern is why the UK's performance since 1965 has been much worse than it was before then, they seem confident that their analysis offers important information on Britain's performance relative to other economies. Thus in addition to presenting a small amount of material on a number of advanced economies (Bacon and Eltis, 1978, ch. 1) the authors have extended their original analysis to include Canada and the US (ibid., ch. 6) and intend to include others.

The defining characteristic of the market sector is that its output is sold in markets at home or overseas. Thus in addition to the private sector of an advanced western economy nationalized industries are included to the extent that they cover costs by sales. In the non-market sector are agents who do not produce marketed output but do exercise claims upon it. Thus this sector comprises non-self-financing public bodies which purchase goods and services from the market sector, and all public employees and recipients of public transfer payments who purchase market sector output to satisfy their consumption requirements. Thus the components of market sector output can be written as follows

$$Y_m \equiv C_m + I_m + C_n + I_n + B_m \qquad (2.8)$$

where Y_m is market sector output, C_m is the consumption of workers in the market sector–the consumption of those who produce marketed output, C_n is marketed output personally consumed and used as raw materials in the non-market sector, I_n is investment in the non-market sector and B_m is the trade balance in marketed output–X_m minus M_m. The market sector includes the manufacturing sector but is much larger than it. In terms of employment the manufacturing sector was roughly 40 per cent of the market sector in the UK in 1973 which in turn accounted for about 80 per cent of total employment.

The authors case for designating the market sector as the key sector for growth is best understood by starting from the following statement:

> suppose an economy . . . has the technological potential to raise its output 5% a year because it can raise output per worker 4% a year and employment 1% a year. If it needs £2 of capital to produce £1 of output . . . [it] can have a 5% rate of growth and a 1% increase in jobs if it invests 10% [of its output] . . . it will only enjoy a 2% rate of growth, and it will lose 2% of its jobs each year if it invests just 4% (Bacon and Eltis, 1978, p. 108).

This of course describes a divergence between the famous 'natural' and 'warranted' growth rates of Harrod. The 'natural' growth rate, which is the sum of the growth rate of labour force (n) and the growth rate of output per worker provided by technical progress (a), is the growth of output which the growth of the resources of labour and technology will sustain and conversely the output growth required to ensure full employment of the growing labour force in the face of labour-saving technical progress. In the quoted example $n + a = 5$ per cent. The assumption that a fixed amount of capital is required to produce one unit of output means that capital requirements for a given level of output Y are $K = vY$ where v is the technologically fixed capital output ratio K/Y. Investment requirements are thus $I = dK/dt = vdY/dt$ and investment requirements for a given growth rate of output are $I/Y = v(dY/dt)(1/Y)$. Conversely the growth rate of output warranted by a given investment ratio is $(dY/dt)(1/Y) = (I/Y)(1/v)$. In the example $v = 2$ and investment requirements for growth at the natural rate are $v(n + a)$ which is ten per cent. A lower investment effort in relation to output at 4 per cent permits an output growth of 2 per cent $(= (I/Y)(1/v))$ which is consistent with expectations of investors but too low to ensure full employment of the growing labour force. Without a greater investment effort a reduction in the volume of capital required to produce each unit of output must be relied on to increase the rate of economic growth and reduce the rate of job loss. This can be accomplished either by a substitution of labour for capital under a given technology or through technical progress of the capital-saving variety. According to the authors the latter is a 'great deal to hope for and the economy will be extremely fortunate if it happens' (Bacon and Eltis, 1978, p. 110), whereas the former will be prevented 'if, as is being assumed here, there are factors which prevent the share of wages from falling' (ibid., p. 199). The upshot of this is that the investment ratio is crucially important for the growth of output and employment.

The importance of the market sector in all this is simply that 'all investment is marketed so . . . must come from the economy's total marketed output' (ibid, p. 28). The market sector is the provider of all physical capital either directly through sales of plant and machinery to domestic firms or indirectly through exports of all goods and services which can finance imports of physical capital from the market sectors of other economies. In general terms the investment ratio will depend on the volume of market sector output relative to claims upon it made by workers in both sectors, public authorities and foreigners. This can be seen by dividing equation (2.8) by Y_m and rearranging

$$i_m \equiv 1 - c_m - c_n - i_n - b_m \qquad (2.9)$$

where all variables are fractions of marketed output. If restrictions are put on the values that c_m and b_m can take i_m will, as a matter of definition, depend inversely on the relative size of the non-market sector as measured by $c_n + i_n$ and thus positively on the relative size of the market sector.[4]

Thus the authors' case for regarding the market sector as the key sector for growth reduces to two hypotheses:

> (1) that the growth rate is determined by the investment ratio; and
> (2) that the investment ratio is determined by the relative size of the non-market (market) sector.

The bulk of the authors' work and the critical comment it has attracted has focused on (2). It is very important to emphasize that (2) does not follow from equation (2.9) which is not an economic hypothesis but a definition which follows directly from the statement in (2.8) of what the components of marketed output are. Thus the authors and their critics have been very much concerned with the conversion of (2.9) into an economic hypothesis and with whether the market sector in the UK has in fact been constrained by the expansion of the non-market sector or by some other cause. However (1) is no less important, for if (2) is correct but (1) is not, the case as presented falls.

In the Harrod model, which the authors employ, the condition for (1) is that $a + n$ is greater than $(I/Y)(1/v)$ – that the natural growth rate exceeds the warranted growth rate. In this case growth proceeds at a rate which is consistent with the expectations of investors (that is at an equilibrium rate) but which is insufficient to prevent growing unemployment, and this rate can be increased by an increase in the investment ratio and reduced by a reduction in it. If the warranted rate is excessive, growth at an equilibrium rate governed by the investment ratio may not be possible. If the warranted rate exceeds the natural rate the actual growth rate must fall short of the warranted rate, for the economy cannot grow through the full employment barrier. The famous instability property of the Harrod model suggests that once this happens there is nothing to prevent growing unemployment and a deepening recession in which the actual growth rate falls further below the warranted rate. Thus growing unemployment is consistent with the warranted rate being greater or less than the natural rate and is not sufficient evidence that the latter is the case. The direct evidence on the relationship between growth rates and investment ratios does not seem to settle this issue in the authors' favour. The result of an OECD (1970, appendix VI) study of 20 advanced economies over the period 1955–67 is that investment ratios are very weakly correlated with growth rates. This is consistent with the conclusion of Beckerman's (1965, ch. 1) earlier analysis that differences between the growth rate of the UK and 11 other advanced economies from 1955 to 1962 are much more associated with differences in the productivity of capital than with differences in investment ratios. The authors' own data for the UK do not provide evidence of a strong positive relationship between the growth rate of marketed output and the investment ratio in the market sector. The results of a linear regression for the UK over the period 1955–1973 are

$$g_{mk} = 9.33 - 1.017i_{mk} \qquad R^2 = 0.1093 \qquad (2.10)$$
$$(0.704)$$

where g_{mk} is the growth rate of net marketed output at 1970 factor cost and i_{mk} is the ratio of net market sector investment excluding dwellings at 1970 factor cost to net marketed output at 1970 factor cost.[5] The standard error is in parentheses. By this test g_{mk} and i_{mk} are almost independent.

The conclusions to be drawn from the arguments reviewed in this chapter are fairly clear-cut. The empirical evidence for Kaldor's argument that manufacturing is the key sector for growth is (1) much stronger than the evidence for Bacon and Eltis's argument on the importance of the market sector (which is very weak in respect of a crucial hypothesis), and

(2) stronger than the evidence for the counter-argument that the expansion of manufacturing has been a result of economic growth. Of course it does not follow from this that the Bacon and Eltis hypothesis that the expansion of the public, non-market, sector can deprive the market sector–including the manufacturing sector–of capital resources is incorrect. The question of whether this has in fact happened in the UK is examined in chapter 4.

Notes

1. See Rowthorn (1975a).
2. See Vaciago (1975).
3. For a survey of the evidence see Thirwall (1980, chs 8 and 9).
4. Many commentators think that the Bacon and Eltis argument implies that non-market expenditures are unproductive. This is incorrect. An increase in I_n or C_n on, say, education can increase the growth rate or labour productivity (a); but this will not result in a higher growth rate of output if the investment share does not also increase.
5. g_{mk} is calculated directly from Bacon and Eltis (1979, appendix A, line 34). i_{mk} is calculated from the same source (lines 28 and 29) and from a price index for net market sector investment excluding dwellings calculated from *National Income Accounts* (1965–75) tables 12.7 and 12.8 and corresponding tables in earlier issues. The period over which the increase in income is measured is 1 year later than that over which the change in the net capital stock is measured.

3 Slow growth and labour shortages

Over the post-war period the growth of manufacturing employment in the UK has been slower than that in any other advanced economy. The magnitudes involved are shown in table 3.1. There are two specific claims in an explanation of UK growth in terms of labour shortages:

(1) that the supply of labour to the growth sector has been the effective constraint on the expansion of advanced economies; and
(2) that this constraint has been tighter in the UK than elsewhere.

Table 3.1
The growth of manufacturing employment, annual average rates

Belgium	(1951–70)	0.49
Canada	(1951–69)	2.20
Denmark	(1957–69)	2.27
France	(1957–69)	1.01
Germany	(1951–70)	2.84
Italy	(1951–70)	2.00
Japan	(1953–69)	4.62
Netherlands	(1951–70)	1.15
Norway	(1951–70)	0.90
UK	(1951–70)	0.39
USA	(1951–69)	1.16

Source: Cornwall (1977b) table 2.

In its time this argument has been supported by two major studies of UK growth. One, by Kaldor, is a direct application to advanced economies of a theory of growth in an under-developed economy. The other, by Denison, uses a hybrid model in which elements drawn from development theory appear alongside concepts describing competitive markets in advanced economies. The argument has also appeared more recently in a different form as a subsidiary part of the Bacon and Eltis thesis that UK growth has been undermined by the expansion of the non-market sector. None of these demon-strations has been successful. Kaldor has renounced his con-clusions on the importance of labour supply and no-one else now takes any variant of the hypothesis very seriously. The history and theoretical basis of the labour shortage argument are nevertheless interesting and worth examining at not too great length.

The claim that a sector within an economy has suffered a shortage of labour requires some account of the conditions which have governed both the demand for labour in the sector and the supply of labour from other sectors. One account of a labour constraint on growth is provided by the theory of dualistic development in an underdeveloped economy. With some difficulty this theory can be stretched to analyse growth in advanced economies.

Surplus labour and labour shortages in an underdeveloped economy

Following Fei and Ranis (1964) the theory envisages an economy of two sectors in which techniques of production are markedly different. In the capitalist (industrial) sector capital machines are used intensively and the level of labour productivity and wages is high. In the subsistence (agricul-tural) sector labour is used intensively and the productivity of workers at the margin is negligible and below the subsis-tence wage. The conditions of agricultural production and employment are shown in figure 3.1. The curve O_aABC shows the total physical product of labour. The marginal productivity of labour diminishes between O_a and B and falls to zero beyond B. Assume that O_aL_1 workers are employed

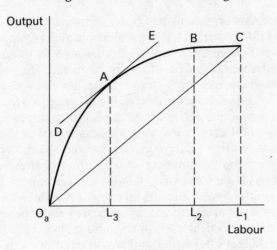

FIGURE 3.1   *The agricultural sector*

to produce a total output L_1C which is just sufficient to meet their subsistence needs. If wages are fixed by an equal shares principle the real wage in agriculture will equal the average productivity of labour – which is equal to the slope of the ray O_aC and greater than the marginal productivity of labour. If this non-market, institutional, wage stays constant as employment is reduced it will continue to exceed the marginal product of labour until employment has contracted to O_aL_3 (until output has contracted to the point on the total product curve where the slope of the tangent to the curve – DAE – equals the slope of O_aC). Any further contraction will drive the marginal product of labour above the institutional wage.

The information in the inverted figure 3.3 is derived directly from figure 3.1 O_aS is the institutional wage which equals L_1C divided by O_aL_1. FGL_2L_1 shows the marginal physical product of labour which is zero and less than O_aS between L_1 and L_2, and positive but less than O_aS between L_2 and L_3. It is clear from an inspection of figure 3.1 that a contraction in agricultural employment from O_aL_1 will generate a surplus of total agricultural output over the consumption requirements of the labour force remaining in agriculture. Between L_1 and L_2 the result of withdrawing an additional worker from agricultural employment is that

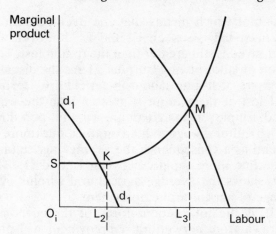

FIGURE 3.2   *The industrial sector*

total output stays constant but wage payments of food fall
by an amount equal to the institutional wage rate. Thus the
agricultural surplus per unit of withdrawn labour – the average agricultural surplus – is equal to O_aS between L and L_2.
A contraction of employment beyond L_2 to L_3 has the same
effect at the margin on wage payments but also reduces total

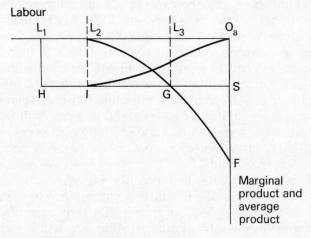

FIGURE 3.3   *The agricultural sector*

agricultural output which means that the average agricultural surplus must fall. Between L_2 and L_3, however, the wage payment saved is still greater than the output lost. This is the condition of labour being 'surplus'. Thus the distance L_1–L_3 is a measure of surplus labour in agriculture. Beyond L_3 the output lost at the margin is greater than the wage payment saved. Employers in agriculture will thus be willing to bid up the agricultural wage to hold on to labour (more of which later) and as a consequence the average agricultural surplus will decline more rapidly between L_3 and O_a. The curve L_1HIO_a shows the average agricultural surplus over the whole range of agricultural employment.

Now if O_aL_1 is the total labour force of the economy, labour withdrawn from agricultural employment will provide both the supply of labour to the industrial sector and the food which industrial workers will require but no longer produce for themselves. The position and slope of the industry labour supply curve is determined by the average agricultural surplus. The industry labour supply curve is the curve SKM in figure 3.2. Between S and K the labour supply to industry is perfectly elastic at the institutional agricultural wage – the average agricultural surplus equals O_aS over this range, thus every worker who migrates to the industrial sector is accompanied by his own food budget. At a given set of relative prices O_aS can be expressed as a real wage in terms of industrial goods measured by O_iS. Alternatively the labour supply curve may be elastic at a real wage higher than O_iS by a margin sufficient to cover the costs of migration. However, beyond K the food available for each additional industrial worker falls at a rate which increases beyond M. The growing shortage of food will cause a rise in the price of food relative to industrial goods and thus a rise in the industrial real wage measured in terms of industrial goods. Thus the industry labour supply curve rises beyond K and rises more steeply beyond M.

All that is needed to complete the model is an industrial demand curve for labour which is simply the curve of the marginal physical product of labour. d_1d_1 is an example. The profit-maximizing level of industrial employment is given by the intersection of SKM and d_1d_1, and industrial profits are shown by the area between the two curves. Growth in the labour surplus economy depends on the rate at which labour is absorbed into the industrial sector, which in turn depends on the expansion of industrial profits and the use to which they are put. The investment of the industrial surplus in machines will shift d_1d_1 to the right by raising the marginal productivity of labour. This effect will be reinforced by dynamic economies of scale in the industrial sector. The rate at which industrial profits expand will fall beyond O_iL_2 as the real industrial wage rises and this in turn will reduce the growth in the demand for industrial labour. Labour absorption will finally stop at O_iL_3. At that point the reserve of surplus labour in agriculture is exhausted and agricultural employers will find it worthwhile to bid against the industrial wage to hold on to labour. Employment in agriculture will now respond to demand factors and will no longer be determined residually as the difference between the total supply of labour and the demand for industrial labour. The two sectors will become competitive and wages will be equalized at marginal products by mobility and profit-maximizing behaviour. 'Labour shortage', what Kaldor calls 'economic maturity', is simply the exhaustion of surplus labour. Thus in terms of figure 3.2 an economy which has attained a distribution of labour O_iL_3/O_aL_3 is suffering from a labour constraint on the growth sector.

The Kaldor–Denison analysis of labour shortages in an advanced economy

The main conclusion of Kaldor's famous inaugural lecture is that 'all countries will experience a slow-down in their growth rates as their agricultural labour reserves become exhausted' (Kaldor, 1966, p. 30).

> Britain, having started the process of industrialization earlier than any other country, has reached 'maturity' much earlier – in the sense that it has attained a distribution of the labour force between the primary, secondary and tertiary sectors at which industry can no longer attract the labour it needs by drawing on the labour reserves of other sectors . . . manpower shortage is the main handicap from which we are suffering (ibid., p. 31).

The conclusion of Denison's equally celebrated analysis of the comparative growth performance of the UK is that

> the most general cause [of higher growth rates in other countries] concerns the gains from reducing waste in the use of resources in agriculture and self employment. The smallness of the contribution to British growth was associated with the amount of waste to be eliminated (Denison, 1967, p. 263).

The Kaldor–Denison conclusion is essentially that the UK ran into labour shortages at a time when all other advanced economies were still enjoying the growth-promoting benefits of surplus labour. Before we look at the evidence that the authors offer for this conclusion it is worth noting that the application of development theory to the problem of growth in advanced economies is in itself controversial. It is difficult to see, for example, that the assumption of the labour surplus model about the technology of agricultural production is appropriate for advanced economies. Output per worker in agriculture has increased in all advanced countries over the post-war period, and in many at a faster rate than productivity growth in industry. In the labour surplus model this results in a continuous shift to the left of the marginal product of labour curve in agriculture (figure 3.3) and of the supply curve of labour to industry (figure 3.2). In other words there is a continuous reduction in the reserve of surplus labour and in the potential for growth from this source. There is also the more general objection that the model is not applicable to advanced economies in which the domain of competitive markets is large and for which neo-classical analysis is more appropriate. In the labour surplus model growth is the result of a continuous reallocation of resources in a non-competitive economy in which the influence of market forces is limited to the advanced sector. In contrast the neo-classical model depicts an integrated system of competitive markets in which factor mobility and profit-maximizing behaviour ensure that factors are rapidly, if not instantaneously, reallocated so as to make marginal products the same in all uses. There is thus no scope for a long-run contribution to growth from the reallocation of existing resources. This implies in turn that growth can only come about through an increase in the volume of factors or an advance in technical knowledge. Those who have applied the concepts of the labour surplus model to the UK and other advanced economies are well aware of this objection. Indeed for some of them the application of the model represents a deliberate assault on neo-classical analysis (see Cripps and Tarling, 1973, introduction and ch. 1; Cornwall, 1977a, ch. 3).

Denison's conclusion emerges from a monumental empirical study which starts from a growth equation specified on neo-classical assumptions of constant returns to scale and perfect competition (that referred to on page 17 above), and which proceeds to use recorded income shares as estimates of the contribution to output growth of changes in the size and quality of the labour force and changes in the size and composition of the capital stock. Neo-classical assumptions are then contradicted, however, by the allowance made for the effects of economies of scale and sectoral shifts in the labour force on productivity growth – the residual between the observed growth of output and the total estimated contribution from the growth of labour and capital. Thus, at the cost of some theoretical inconsistency, Denison's analysis allows precise statements to be made about the absolute and relative importance of a large number of different sources of growth of which the reallocation of labour from agriculture to industry is just one.[1] The quantitative importance of labour reallocation depends on a set of assumptions about output gains and losses resulting from labour movements between sectors.[2] The estimating technique is to multiply the assumed net change in output per worker by the number of workers who moved from agricultural to non-agricultural employment. Denison's finding is that for the period 1950–62 the largest single source of the difference in growth performance between the UK and eight other advanced economies is the greater economies of scale enjoyed by other economies: this factor accounted for 21 per cent of the total difference between the average growth rate of the UK and the average growth rates of all other economies in the sample. This figure is greater than the proportion attributable to the reallocation to industry of greater labour reserves in agriculture (19.7 per cent) only because of the exceptionally large contribution of economies of scale in one other economy – Western Germany. The reallocation of larger reserves of labour from non-farm self-employment accounted for an additional 6.2 per cent of the observed difference between UK growth and growth in all other economies.

As Kaldor's starting position is that the neo-classical paradigm is false his conclusion on the importance of surplus labour is theoretically unambiguous. The specific empirical evidence cited in support of it consists of two items. The first is the regression result reported in chapter 2 (equations (2.4) and (2.5)) that the growth of productivity generated by the growth of manufacturing output is not sufficient to avoid the need for a growth of employment. The second is that over the period 1954–64 the UK experienced a growth rate of industrial employment lower than that in 11 other advanced economies and had the smallest proportion of the labour force in the primary sector (agriculture and mining). The precise figures are in Kaldor (1966), tables 3 and 4. Unlike Denison's investigation, Kaldor's analysis does not provide quantitative statements of the importance of labour reallocation relative to other factors. It is however clear that Kaldor attaches some importance to demand factors and to the 'interaction between increases in demand induced by increases in supply and of increases in supply generated in response to increases in demand' (Kaldor, 1966, p. 19).

The Bacon and Eltis analysis of labour shortages

The main plank of the Bacon and Eltis thesis is an argument about the relationship between the non-market sector and profits, investment and growth in the market sector. The authors do, however, have a supporting argument about labour shortages caused by the expansion of the non-market sector in the UK. The argument has no great theoretical complexity and can be stated very simply: increases in public sector employment have been used as a cheap and flexible policy during periods of recession but 'the increase in employment to provide more public services continued through boom and recession, and until 1975, each increase was permanent; so the workers taken on in recession were not available to industry in subsequent booms' (Bacon and Eltis, 1978, p. 15). The evidence for this argument is that, over the period 1961–75,

> (1) the 41 per cent increase in ratio of non-industrial employment to industrial employment in the UK was much greater than that experienced in Germany (32.8 per cent), the US (27.9 per cent), France (22.5 per cent), Italy (12.6 per cent) and Japan (4.5 per cent) (ibid., chart 7), and
> (2) the increase in UK non-industrial service employment in central government (26.5 per cent) and local government (69.7 per cent) was much greater than the increase in private sector service employment (10.5 per cent) (ibid., chart 8).

An assessment

The Bacon and Eltis formulation of the labour shortage hypothesis does not stand up to close scrutiny. In a detailed study Jackson (1977) has shown that the ratio of public sector employment to total employment in the UK has remained almost constant between 1959 and 1974. Of course evidence on movements in the aggregate ratio is not conclusive, for labour shortages could have arisen from the expansion of a particular skill, age or sex category of public employment which deprived the manufacturing sector of the sort of labour it required for expansion. Such evidence as exists on this issue does not support the Bacon and Eltis position. Over the period 1966–76 72 per cent of the fall in employment in UK production industries consisted of males whereas 74 per cent of the increase in employment in the public sector consisted of females many of whom were part-time (see Thatcher, 1979, table 2.4). Thus what seems to have happened is that additional public demand for labour has been largely met by a higher female participation rate and not by a squeeze on manpower in manufacturing.

The more fully fledged arguments of Kaldor and Denison cannot be disposed of so easily. It is important to see that the hypothesis presented by Kaldor and used by Denison says something more than that an expansion of industry and manufacturing requires more labour. The argument that the supply of labour has been an effective constraint means that limitations in the supply of labour frustrated an expansion of manufacturing employment and output that would have otherwise taken place. Or to put it another way, that an expansion of the labour supply was a necessary and sufficient condition for an expansion of manufacturing. Thus the counter-arguments which the hypothesis must reject is that the expansion of manufacturing employment was governed by the growth of demand for manufacturing output and that a more abundant supply of labour to manufacturing would have merely resulted in higher unemployment. Spelling out the hypothesis fully makes it clear that evidence on employment cannot settle the issue one way or the other. Kaldor's finding that a growth of manufacturing output of 1 per cent requires an increase in employment of $\frac{1}{2}$ per cent is consistent with the expansion of manufacturing having been governed by supply factors, including but not necessarily confined to labour shortages, or by demand factors, or by some more complex interaction of the two. Evidence on the growth and distribution of employment by sectors is inconclusive for the same reason. Denison's findings are equally inconclusive. The finding that other economies gained much more from labour reallocations than the UK does not demonstrate that expansion in the UK would have been greater had the reserves of labour available for reallocation been greater than they actually were. Larger numbers in agriculture and self-employment may just have stayed put as a result of slow expansion of demand for manufacturing output. The difficulty here is a straightforward problem of identification which cannot be resolved without a less ambiguous form of evidence. There are a few more useful items of evidence specific to the UK. Some of them relate only to a part of the post-war period and none of them taken separately is conclusive, but when taken together they make it very difficult to argue that UK manufacturing industry has suffered from a chronic shortage of manpower. Thus UK manufacturers have been continuously releasing labour since the mid-1960s – Thatcher's (1979) survey shows a fall in manufacturing employment of almost 16 per cent between 1966 and 1976. Also during the early 1960s the UK displayed a very low propensity to employ labour available to the non-agricultural sector in manufacturing – Cornwall's analysis (1977a, p. 91) shows that between 1960 and 1965 only 20 out of every 100 workers becoming available for non-agricultural employment in the UK were employed in manufacturing (and only 24 were employed in industry as a whole including manufacturing); these figures compare with 28 (47) in France, 33 (45) in Germany and 38 (47) in Japan. In addition to this there is evidence that substantial reserves of labour have existed within UK manufacturing in the form of overmanning (CPRS, 1975; Pratten and Atkinson, 1976). It is on the basis of evidence such as this that Kaldor (1975b) has renounced the main conclusion of his inaugural lecture.

This evidence suggests but does not prove that the growth of manufacturing employment in the UK has been governed by demand rather than supply factors. More systematic evidence on the relative importance of supply and demand factors is very thin on the ground. Empirical studies on the supply of labour have concentrated almost exclusively on the determinants of participation rates by age and sex, and provide very little information on supply conditions in economic sectors. Also almost all results have been derived from single equation models in which 'no explicit attention is given to the fact that the demand for labour also helps determine the . . . observations . . . of employment' (Byers, 1976, pp. 87 and 88). The only systematic comparative study of the importance of supply and demand factors for the growth of manufacturing employment is that by Parikh cited in chapter 2, the conclusion of which is that 'growth in employment in the manufacturing sector is determined by the growth of manufacturing output while the growth in output is . . . determined by the growth in exports in that sector' (Parikh, 1978, p. 86). This conclusion, unlike many others advanced in this area, is based on an analysis which explicitly recognizes the identification problem. As a postscript to this review of evidence it should be said that shortages of certain categories of skilled labour do appear to have held back manufacturing expansion in the UK during cyclical up-swings – for example in 1973. This has, however, been a purely short-term phenomenon with at most extremely limited significance for growth in the long run.

The overall conclusion which emerges from the evidence is that neither the earlier contraction of agricultural employment nor the more recent expansion of public sector employment has been an effective constraint on the expansion of manufacturing in the UK. The available evidence, which is not particularly abundant or systematic, suggests that the expansion of employment in UK manufacturing is better understood as having been dependent on the expansion of demand for manufactured goods.

Notes

1. It is not possible to give a detailed account of Denison's estimation technique in a short survey. Estimates are made of the contribution of over 20 different factors to the observed difference between the growth rate of the UK and growth rates in eight other economies. Recorded income shares are not used for all estimates and in some cases pragmatic judgements are used.
2. The assumption on the loss of agricultural output is that it is one-quarter of the percentage reduction in farm employment in all countries except the USA, UK and Denmark – in which it is one-third, and Italy – in which it is zero. Denison assumes that the percentage gain in non-farm output is four-fifths of the percentage growth in the non-farm labour force resulting from the shift of labour out of agriculture for all countries except the USA and Italy, in which the gain is three-quarters.

4 Slow growth and capital shortages

The evidence most frequently appealed to in arguments about UK growth is probably that on industrial investment and profitability. By any conventional measure the investment performance of the UK manufacturing sector has been inferior to that achieved elsewhere. Table 4.1 shows the record in terms of growth rates and levels per employee. The picture does not change if performance is measured instead by the share of manufacturing investment in manufacturing output.

International figures are not available on the definition of profits relevant to decisions on investment – that is gross profits minus depreciation at current costs, stock appreciation and tax liabilities. The record in table 4.2 on gross rates of

Table 4.1
Gross manufacturing investment, 1960–72 and 1973

	UK	Germany	France	USA	Japan	Italy
Annual growth rate 1960–72	2.64	2.99	7.84	6.00	11.14	2.99
Per employee, in US dollars						
1960	334	—	—	—	492	332
1965	460	—	905	1675	460	367
1973	751	1658	2182	2551	2147	1224

Source: NEDO (1975) table 2.2 and Brown and Sheriff (1979) table 10.9.

Table 4.2
Corporate profitability

	UK	Germany	France	USA	Japan	Italy
Gross rate of return						
1960	5.8	13.1	9.5	15.3	—	5.6
1965	5.4	11.7	9.2	18.8	11.9	5.3
1973	3.1	11.5	9.6	14.7	10.9	4.0
Gross profit share in value added						
1963	23.3	27.2	29.1	28.1	41.6	30.0
1965	22.3	27.2	29.2	29.5	39.7	31.6
1973	16.8	26.1	31.9	25.0	36.8	25.4

Source: OECD (1977) pp. 305–7.

return and shares of gross profits in value added shows that corporate profitability in the UK has been at a lower level and declined more sharply than elsewhere.

The interpretation that many place on this evidence is that industrial expansion in the UK has been restricted by a shortage of the profits required to finance investment. This proposition is central to the Bacon and Eltis (1978) thesis and to an earlier analysis of UK economic performance since the war by Glyn and Sutcliffe (1972). The emphasis which these authors give to the link between financial factors and investment also appears in the arguments of those who attribute the poor investment performance of the UK to the failures and inefficiencies of its financial institutions. An assessment of these arguments involves an examination of the form and strength of the causal links between profits, finance and investment. This takes us into difficult territory for theoretical models of the determinants of investment are not easily formulated and tested. For this reason it is useful to provide an explicit framework for assessment by sketching out an investment model in which the effects of profits, finance and other factors can be seen. Although complex investment models have been developed[1], a fairly simple model incorporating schedules for the marginal cost of investment funds and the marginal efficiency of investment is sufficient for this purpose.

A model of investment

Investment can be financed internally from undistributed profits and externally from fixed interest loans and share issues; but the risk of bankruptcy rises with rising debt interest charges, and managerial control is diluted by an increase in the number of outstanding shares. Thus the cost imputed to external finance is higher than that imputed to internal finance and rises as more external finance is used. This idea is expressed in the rising marginal cost of funds schedule shown in figure 4.1. OA measures the foregone interest imputed to ploughed-back profits. The slope of the schedule in the region of external finance is determined by the terms on which external finance is available and the whole schedule will shift in response to changes in realized profits (more of which later).

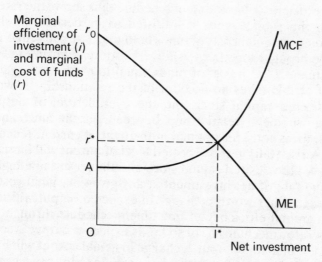

FIGURE 4.1   *The marginal cost of funds and the marginal efficiency of investment*

Net investment (gross investment minus depreciation) is the means by which the actual capital stock is adjusted to the desired capital stock. An increase in the rate of net investment will drive up the price of capital goods – unless the supply of capital goods is perfectly elastic – and thus reduce the expected rate of return to investment (the marginal efficiency of investment). In this case there will be a negative relationship between the marginal efficiency of investment and the rate of net investment and the greater the rise in the price of capital goods the steeper will be the negative slope of the marginal efficiency of investment schedule. The position of the schedule will depend on the size of the existing capital stock and on the state of expectations about the rate of return to investment. Thus if expected returns are some function of actual profits a rise (fall) in realized profits will shift the schedule to the right (left). It will be profitable to undertake net investment whenever the marginal efficiency of investment (i) is greater than the prevailing marginal cost of investment funds (r). Thus in figure 4.1 if $r = r_0$ the profit-maximizing rate of net investment is zero which means that the capital stock is at its desired level. The marginal efficiency of investment schedule thus shows the rate at which the capital stock is adjusted to its desired level at different marginal costs of funds below r_0. The two schedules can be brought together to show a profit maximizing rate of investment I^* at a cost of funds equal to r^*.

All of this takes no account of the relationship between the desired capital stock and the overall level of output. There will be a relationship between output and capital which firms consider optimal in the light of current technology. A rise (fall) in the expected level of output will increase (reduce) the desired capital stock and thus result in a higher (lower) rate of net investment at any given marginal cost of funds. In other words a change in expected output will shift the marginal efficiency of investment schedule through the accelerator mechanism. In so far as expected output is some function of actual output, a change in actual output will have a similar effect on the schedule as a change in realized profits.

Bacon and Eltis, and Glyn and Sutcliffe, on the investment squeeze

The Bacon and Eltis thesis is a conversion of the identity

$$i_m \equiv 1 - c_m - c_n - i_n - b_m \qquad (4.1)$$

(introduced on page 39) into the economic hypothesis that the investment ratio in the market sector depends inversely on the relative size of the non-market sector. The hypothesis rests on two propositions;

> (1) that the increase in taxation required to finance an increase in the non-market share will (a) reduce post-tax profits but (b) not reduce the investment ratio required for full employment growth[2]; and
> (2) that falling post-tax profits will reduce the actual investment ratio.

The authors find it difficult to specify a plausible theoretical model of income distribution and capital accumulation which will generate both of these results. The general assumptions on which the theoretical analysis proceeds are that non-market expenditure is financed by revenues from a proportional tax levied at an equal rate on wages and profits, and that, as a matter of policy, the balance of trade in marketed output is maintained at zero. The second assumption (that b_m equals zero in equation (4.1)) ensures that the additional resources absorbed by a larger non-market sector will not be provided by foreigners. The struggle is thus between firms and workers in the market sector. The analysis centres on the effects on income distribution, profits and investment of an increase in the non-market share and thus in the proportional rate of tax; the crucial factors being the extent to which profits are vulnerable to attempts by workers to shift higher taxation from wages onto profits by raising wages, and the effects on investment of changes in profits. The authors show that in a neo-classical model of distribution (that is one in which income shares are determined by the equilibrium quantities and prices of factors established in perfectly competitive factor markets) in which the factor mix is independent of relative factor prices an increase in the tax rate leaves the profit share net of tax undisturbed. The effect of a higher tax rate on profits is exactly offset by an increase in the profits share before tax which results from the passing on of profits taxation in the form of higher prices. The extra cost of the larger non-market sector is borne entirely by workers in the market sector who pay a higher rate of tax on a smaller income share before tax. In terms of equation (4.1) this result is one in which the rise in c_n plus i_n is exactly offset by a fall in c_m with i_m undisturbed, which is precisely the result the authors do not wish to demonstrate. In a neo-classical model in which the factor mix depends on relative factor prices an increase in the tax rate is associated with a reduced profits share net of tax but also with a lower required investment ratio. Thus propositions (1a) and (2) can be demonstrated but not (1b). A simple non-competitive model of distribution brings the authors no nearer to the required results. In a model in which pre-tax income shares depend on the relative monopoly power of labour and capital, and monopoly power does not depend on the relative size of the non-market sector, the extra cost of the larger non-market sector is shown to fall equally on wages and profits. For, with no change in the balance of monopoly power, profit-earners (and wage-earners) are unable to offset the effects of higher taxation by shifting the pre-tax distribution of income in their own favour. However, the fall in the profits share net of tax will not reduce the investment ratio if firms are able and willing to raise more external finance by borrowing from the government and from workers. The authors argue that this may not be possible if

> (1) the reduced income share of workers net of tax implies a consumption share below 'a Malthusian lower limit to workers consumption' (Bacon and Eltis, 1978, p. 185); and
> (2) firms are already close to the maximum ratio of fixed interest debt to equity which they find acceptable – that is close to their gearing limits.

In the case of (1) workers are assumed to bid for compensation by wage inflation which firms are unable to resist by price inflation. The authors believe that workers in the UK have exploited two specific advantages in this struggle: the vulnerability to industrial disruption of firms introducing new high-cost plant, and legislation on matters such as redundancy which has changed property rights in favour of workers. Thus

> workers can pass on taxes by causing exceptional wage inflation that leads to a squeeze on profit margins, either because prices and incomes policies are introduced to control inflation which impose lower profit margins on companies, or because the exchange rate is not lowered in line with domestic inflation with the result that international competition squeezes profit margins (ibid., 1978, pp. 98 and 99).

The result is that the pre-tax distribution of income shifts in favour of workers which further reduces profits net of tax. In the case of (2) firms will be unable to

> make up through borrowing the finance they no longer obtain through profits . . . indeed they will have to borrow less than in the past . . . investment will be doubly reduced (ibid., p. 105).

The imposition of these two conditions on a non-competitive model of distribution and accumulation completes the authors' rather tortuous demonstration of the theory of an inverse causal relationship between $\dot{c}_n + i_n$ and i_m. In terms of the investment model outlined in the previous section the Bacon and Eltis thesis is essentially that a government-induced profits squeeze has reduced investment by shifting the marginal cost of funds schedule to the left through a shortening of the elastic section of the curve representing undistributed profits.

The empirical support for the thesis consists of evidence for the UK on the share in net marketed output of non-market purchases – rising from 33.3 per cent in 1955 to 39.8 per cent in 1973 (Bacon and Eltis, 1979, pp. 413 and 414); the share of net manufacturing profits in manufacturing value added – falling from 14.9 per cent in 1961 to 7.2 per cent in 1973 (Bacon and Eltis, 1978, table 11.3); and the share of net market sector fixed investment in net marketed output – 5.6 per cent in 1955, 7.7 per cent in 1961 and 7.2 per cent in 1973. Over the same period the share of net industrial fixed investment fell much more sharply from 4.6 per cent in 1961 to 2 per cent in 1973 (Bacon and Eltis, 1979, pp. 413 and 414). The evidence provided by international comparisons (Bacon and Eltis, 1978, ch. 6) is less positive. Over the period 1955–75 non-market spending in Canada and the US increased faster as a share of marketed output than in the UK but the outcomes were very different. In the US the rising non-market share displaced both consumption and investment in the market sector, whereas in Canada the non-market sector grew entirely at the expense of consumption in the market sector, the fall in which was sufficiently large to allow a simultaneous increase in the share of market investment.

The Bacon and Eltis thesis has several elements in common with the analysis of post-war British capitalism by Glyn and Sutcliffe (1972) the central argument of which is that profitability in the UK has been reduced to a critical level by wage inflation which firms have been unable to resist by increasing prices because of increasing competition in international markets. The authors' analysis of the effects of narrowing profit margins is very similar to that of Bacon and Eltis although they give more emphasis to the effects of profitability on investment expectations. Thus

> the amount of investing done by companies depends a lot on their relative profitability . . . profits influence expectations about the likely profitability of new investment and . . . they are the main source of finance' (Glyn and Sutcliffe, 1972, p. 120)

> . . . there are limits to how far companies can go in increasing their long term debt relative to their total assets . . . a depression of the stock market resulting from low profitability will also inhibit share issues . . . in this way the need for external finance and the difficulty of raising it will increase together (ibid., pp. 123 and 124).

Where the two theses differ is in their analysis of the cause of the profits squeeze. For Bacon and Eltis the autonomous cause is the expansion of government economic activity, whereas for Glyn and Sutcliffe the primary causes are the increasing offensive strength of workers resulting from two decades of full employment and a progressive fall in the price and cost competitiveness of UK goods in world markets. For Glyn and Sutcliffe, with one or two minor exceptions, the role of government has been to intervene in this struggle on the side of profits and investment with a support operation based on a wide range of policies on taxation, public expenditure, the exchange rate and wages and industrial relations.

In terms of the investment model the Glyn and Sutcliffe thesis is that a profits squeeze resulting from increased worker militancy and international competition has shifted both the marginal cost of funds schedule and the marginal efficiency of investment schedule to the left. The main items of evidence offered in support of this thesis are figures on the steadily falling share of profits in company net output between 1950 and 1970 (ibid., table 3.2); the steadily falling rate of profit net of tax in industry and commerce between 1965 and 1970 (ibid., table 3.3); and the steady fall in the proportion of industrial and commercial finance provided by retained earnings and depreciation allowances between 1950 and 1970 (ibid., table 6.1).

An inefficient financial system

The idea that finance is vital for investment has motivated several lengthy investigations of the efficiency of the UK financial system. The issue is examined in great detail in NEDO (1975), Samuel, Groves and Goddard (1975) and most recently in the report of the Wilson Committee (Cmnd 7937, 1980). The allegation which such inquiries have examined is simply that the peculiar institutional structure and motives of the UK financial system have deprived the industrial sector of investment finance.

In the minds of the advocates of this view has usually been a model of a superior growth-promoting system of financial institutions which exists in no one other country but contains elements of the arrangements in Germany, France, Italy and

Japan. A fairly representative statement of the argument can be found in the Labour Party pamphlet (1976). The ideal system is one in which public or semi-public banks and insurance companies purchase equity stakes in manufacturing companies and are the main channel through which investment funds are directed into the manufacturing sector from elsewhere. Such institutions provide medium- and long-term finance for industrial investment on low-security ratios and with generous payback periods. The commonly cited examples include the nationalized banks in France – the Banque Nationale de Paris, the Crédit Lyonnais and the Société Générale – and the state-owned Caisse de Dépôts des Consignations which channels funds from French savings banks and insurance companies; the Italian IRI state holding company which controls operating companies in telecommunications, shipping, shipbuilding, steel and engineering and owns three of the largest national banks; and the Japanese trading conglomerates and Trust Fund Bureau which is an equivalent of the French CDC. Against this model the multiple deficiencies of the UK financial system become clear. Supine and conservative private insurance companies and pension funds have come to dominate the UK system and for reasons not usually explained are inclined

> (1) to invest in land, property and art works rather than in new capital machinery;
> (2) to demand relatively high security ratios and short payback periods in making loans for new investment; and
> (3) to invest overseas.

The result of this has been a shortage of external finance for manufacturing companies which has held back investment. Put in terms of the investment model this argument amounts to the claim that for institutional reasons the upward-sloping section of the marginal cost of funds schedule has drifted upwards in the UK and has been higher than elsewhere. The evidence cited in support of this argument usually consists of figures on investment performance such as those in table 4.1 and measures of gearing ratios which show the UK ratio to have been lower than that in other advanced economies.

An assessment

Each argument outlined in the previous section has difficulties specific to it. An implication of the Labour Party view of the UK financial system is that financial institutions have repeatedly neglected profitable investment opportunities. How is it that they have not learned by their mistakes? The fact that the entire weight of the Bacon and Eltis thesis is carried by two *ad hoc* assumptions has led two observers to conclude that 'their basic model . . . has to be twisted and loaded with unsubstantiated subsidiary assumptions if it is to yield results compatible with [the] thesis' (Hadjimatheou and Skouras, 1979, p. 396). Glyn and Sutcliffe ask but do not answer the question why the UK has faced an increasing degree of international competition.

There is, however, a single objection to each of the arguments. Despite the important differences between them the arguments rely on a common theory of investment in which profits and finance are the independent explanatory variables. The objection to them is simply that the primary determinant of investment in the UK has been the achieved expansion of demand and output acting through the accelerator mechanism. In this case the squeeze on profits and finance and the slow rate of investment are associated together only as the joint products of a slow expansion of manufacturing output and not, as the above arguments suppose, as cause and effect. Or, to put the point more generally, the supply of investment finance depends on the rate of economic expansion and not the reverse. To protect itself from this charge the capital shortage hypothesis must insist on a counter-factual claim equivalent to that implied in the labour shortage hypothesis: that, all other things unchanged, more profits and finance would have generated more investment. It is not enough for the advocates of the hypothesis to show that profits, finance and investment moved in the same direction because this outcome is consistent with both the thesis and the antithesis.

The obvious question now is to ask whether the evidence provided by formal studies of investment behaviour supports the profits–finance theory or the accelerator theory.

Changes in capacity utilization and output have been found to be highly significant determinants of industrial investment in the UK in studies by Nobay (1970), Junankar (1970), Smyth and Briscoe (1969) and Panić and Vernon (1975). It has proved much more difficult to establish the importance of financial factors measured by interest rates, the user cost of capital and profits.[3] The influence of interest rates on fixed industrial investment in the UK has not been clearly demonstrated. A study by Feldstein and Fleming (1971) shows an interest rate variable to be statistically insignificant but Hines and Catephores (1970) show a significant interest rate effect. Feldstein and Fleming (1971) and Nobay (1970) show a composite user cost of capital variable to be statistically significant but relatively unimportant in explaining variations in investment. However, the results of more recent research in the Bank of England on the relationship between investment and the ratio of the cost of capital to the rate of return on capital 'have not been particularly encouraging . . . though in some cases [the ratio] has proved to be just as successful as conventional accelerator models in explaining the behaviour of investment' (Bank of England, 1977, p. 157). Nobay (1970) finds that profits have had a relatively small but significant effect on manufacturing investment excluding chemicals and steel (but no significant effect on total manufacturing investment) but are highly correlated with output and capacity utilization. Panić and Vernon (1975) also find no significant relationship between profits entered as a proxy for internal sources of finance and total manufacturing investment.

It may be that these varied and inconclusive results on the influence of financial variables arise partly from the difficulty of accurately measuring the marginal cost of capital funds. It should also be said that tests on US data have usually shown fixed investment to be more sensitive to financial variables (see for example Fromm, 1971) although the importance of profits seems to be confined to the timing of investment expenditures in the short run. There is also the general reservation that the results of these studies are provided by estimates of the parameters of single-equation models which will be misleading if simultaneous effects are present. This said, however, we must make use of what we know. Unavailable evidence may tell a different story, but the information we have is that output and capacity utilization are powerful explanatory variables whereas the effects of financial variables are erratic and typically never more than weak. How far does this conclusion support a fundamental objection to the capital shortage hypothesis? What can be said is that the weight which the hypothesis puts on the profits–finance theory of investment is very much greater than the available evidence will support. The positive counter-argument that the main causal factor has been the expansion of demand and output achieved is much more consistent with the evidence provided by existing studies. The onus of proof is thus firmly on those who would dispute the argument that low investment and profitability have been a symptom of slow industrial expansion in the UK and not a cause of it.

Notes

1. For a very clear introduction to modern theories of investment behaviour see Junankar (1972).
2. As the required investment share equals $v(a + n)$ – see chapter 2 page 38 – and $a + n$ assumed to be independent of $c_n + i_n$, this reduces to the proposition that an increase in the tax rate will not be associated with a reduction in v.
3. For a survey of UK studies of the impact of financial factors on investment see Savage (1978).

5 Slow productivity growth

There is a consensus amongst investigators that differences in national growth rates have more to do with differential growth rates of factor productivity than with differential growth rates of factor inputs; but agreement on this exists only at a general and qualitative level. There is active disagreement, or at least no settled view, both on the correct definition and measure of factor productivity and on the causes of productivity growth. A major difficulty in the analysis of causes is to identify the nature and size of the contribution of the elusive agent of technical progress. For an economy described by equation (5.1) in which output depends on capital, labour and the level of technology – measured by an index T:

$$Y = F(K, L, T) \qquad (5.1)$$

an obvious definition of productivity is output per unit of total labour and capital input. Apart from the difficulty of measuring the capital input and constructing an index of both inputs, however, this definition makes less sense if capital accumulation is a consequence rather than a cause of output growth. Whatever definition is adopted the major issue still remains: what determines the rate of growth of productivity? How important is technical progress as against improvements in efficiency which allow more to be produced from given resources of labour and capital in the absence of technical progress? Is the contribution from technical progress endogenous or exogenous – in other words have differences in technical progress between economies been largely a result or byproduct of differences in achieved rates of growth, or have they arisen more or less independently to produce the differences in growth that can be observed? In order to define these issues more precisely and to identify the evidence relevant to them a simple model of productivity growth is developed in the next section. This model incorporates a number of elements which have been examined in earlier chapters – namely technical inefficiency, endogenous technical progress and endogenous capital accumulation – and which are realistic features of advanced economies.

A model of productivity growth

Assuming that capital and labour are substitutable, that increases in capital, labour and technical progress are independent, and that technical progress is exogenous, the aggregate production function shown in equation (5.1) yields the standard growth equation

$$g_y = \alpha g_k + \beta g_l + \lambda_x \qquad (5.2)$$

in which λ_x represents the contribution to output growth of the exogenously given growth rate of the index of technology. For ease of exposition assume that the capital and labour elasticities sum to one. Equations (5.1) and (5.2) assume that available supplies of capital and labour are fully utilized. In the long run, however, spare capacity may exist and the level of utilization of factors may change. Variations in capacity utilization are obviously to be expected in the short run as the pressure of demand changes over the cycle, but other factors may operate along a path of long-run growth at a constant pressure of demand. Changes in worker and management practices may result in a more efficient use of existing resources under a given state of technology. Thus changes in rules and informal codes governing, for example, the demarcation of jobs and negotiating procedures between workers and management may increase the output produced from each machine (reduce underproduction) and reduce the number of man-hours required to operate each machine (reduce overmanning). Following Gomulka (1979) this idea can be expressed by rewriting equation (5.1) as

$$Y = F(K \cdot u_k, L \cdot u_l, T) \tag{5.3}$$

where u_k and u_l are the utilization rates of capital and labour which can take values between 0 and 1. Equation (5.2) now becomes

$$g_y = \alpha(g_k + g_{uk}) + (1 - \alpha) (g_l + g_{ul}) + \lambda_x \tag{5.4}$$

where g_{uk} and g_{ul} are the growth rates of u_k and u_l, and $1 - \alpha$ is written for β. Note that utilization rates affect the overall growth rate only to the extent that they change.

A contribution from endogenous technical progress can be allowed for by relaxing the assumption that capital accumulation and technical progress are independent and introducing the learning hypothesis examined in chapter 1. The rate of labour augmenting technical progress depends on increasing experience measured by the growth rate of the capital stock, and the rate of learning from experience measured by the elasticity of output per worker with respect to capital (m) which is assumed to be positive but less than 1. Thus

$$\lambda_e = g_k \cdot m. \tag{5.5}$$

Recall from chapter 2 that this form of technical progress is the same thing as Kaldor's dynamic economies of scale. Equation (5.4) is now rewritten as

$$g_y = \alpha (g_k + g_{uk}) + (1 - \alpha)(g_l + g_{ul} + g_k \cdot m) + \lambda_x. \tag{5.6}$$

The second term on the right-hand side shows that the growth of the effective labour force is a combination of increases in the number of workers, the efficiency of work and the skill of workers.

The dependence of capital accumulation on output growth can be expressed by the simple accelerator relationship introduced in chapter 1. Thus

$$K = vY, \qquad (5.7)$$

which implies that $g_k = g_y$. Substituting g_y for g_k in (5.6) and rearranging gives

$$g_y = g_y(\alpha + m(1 - \alpha)) + \alpha g_{uk} + (1 - \alpha)(g_l + g_{ul}) + \lambda_x. \qquad (5.8)$$

Thus

$$g_y = \frac{\alpha g_{uk} + (1 - \alpha)g_{ul}}{(1 - \alpha)(1 - m)} + \frac{(1 - \alpha)g_l}{(1 - \alpha)(1 - m)} + \frac{\lambda_x}{(1 - \alpha)(1 - m)}. \qquad (5.9)$$

The mechanism of output growth is now quite complex. Increases in utilization rates, the labour force and exogenous technical progress have direct impacts on the growth rate – measured by αg_{uk}, $(1 - \alpha)g_{ul}$, $(1 - \alpha)g_l$ and λ_x respectively. However, any factor which increases output also stimulates capital accumulation through the accelerator mechanism which further increases output through the output–capital elasticity coefficient (α) and through the learning function which converts a faster rate of capital accumulation into a faster rate of endogenous technical progress. In this way increases in g_{uk}, g_{ul}, g_l and λ_x generate feedback effects between g_y, g_k and λ_e which serve to multiply all direct contributions by $1/[(1 - \alpha)(1 - m)]$. The higher are the values of α and m the greater is the growth multiplier.

An expression for productivity growth can easily be derived from (5.9). The second term on the right-hand side of the equation can be rewritten as $g_l + [(g_l \cdot m)/(1 - m)]$ which after rearrangement gives

$$g_y - g_l = \frac{\alpha g_{uk} + (1 - \alpha)g_{ul}}{(1 - \alpha)(1 - m)} + \frac{g_l \cdot m}{(1 - m)}$$

$$+ \frac{\lambda_x}{(1 - \alpha)(1 - m)}. \qquad (5.10)$$

This equation shows that in an economy in which capital accumulation is endogenous the correct measure of productivity growth is the growth of output per worker. The indirect influence of capital accumulation is captured through the growth multiplier. The right-hand side of (5.10) shows that the growth rate of labour productivity will be faster

> (1) the faster are inefficiencies eliminated in the use of capital and labour (the higher are g_{uk} and g_{ul});
> (2) the faster is the rate of learning from experience (m) and thus the faster is the rate of endogenous technical progress; and
> (3) the faster is the rate of exogenous technical progress (λ_x).

The international record of productivity growth in manufacturing is shown in table 5.1. The explanation of the UK

Table 5.1
Growth rates of output per worker in manufacturing, 1951–73*
(percentages)

	1951–56	1956–60	1960–64	1964–69	1969–73
France	4.37	4.03	4.68	5.42	4.58
Germany	5.48	5.06	4.37	4.88	4.37
Italy	5.95	5.09	4.31	5.63	4.14
Japan	7.54	8.96	7.27	10.40	10.30
Netherlands	4.32	4.65	3.94	7.19	7.11
UK	2.59	2.08	2.79	3.71	4.46

	1951–56	1956–66	1966–69	1969–73
Belgium	3.22	4.95	4.73	4.62
Canada	3.83	2.50	1.99	4.00
USA	1.85	3.20	1.74	4.16

Sources: Cripps and Tarling (1973); Brown and Sheriff (1979)
    *The terminal years for individual countries are as shown above except for the following:

France	1951–57, 1957–60
Germany	1956–61, 1961–65
Italy	1951–55, 1955–59; 1959–63; 1963–70
Japan	1953–57, 1957–61, 1961–64
Netherlands	1960–65, 1965–70
UK	1951–55, 1955–60, 1960–65, 1965–69
Belgium	1951–57, 1957–64, 1964–70.

record suggested by the model above is that compared to most other advanced economies the UK suffered from increasing relative inefficiency, or a slower rate of endogenous technical progress, or a slower rate of exogenous technical progress, or of course some combination of all three.

Inefficiency in the UK

Amongst pundits there is a widespread belief that in the UK less efficient use is made of available resources than elsewhere. This belief is much stronger than the evidence available to support it. There is no shortage of evidence that the level of labour productivity in UK manufacturing has been lower than elsewhere, but it is very difficult to be sure that this represents greater inefficiency in the UK rather than inferior technology and capital equipment with no difference in utilization rates. Pratten and Atkinson (1976) give a brief survey of studies which have attempted to disentangle the cause of the low level of productivity in UK manufacturing. Most investigators have simply asked firms about the different causes of low productivity. A major drawback of this method is that the answers received to not usually provide a quantitative estimate of the importance of inefficiency; but this said it is difficult, if not impossible, to devise a quantitative index of worker and management practices which would allow such estimates to be made. The qualitative conclusion which emerges from most studies is that inefficiencies in the use of manpower have been one cause of a lower productivity level but that inferior capital equipment and a smaller scale of production have been equally important.

The level of inefficiency, however, will have no influence on the growth rate of productivity unless it changes (in which case g_{uk} and, or, g_{ul} in equation (5.10) will take non-zero values), or unless there is a relationship between efficiency and productivity other than that described by utilization rates (in which case equation (5.10) does not give a complete account of productivity growth). There is no evidence whatsoever that the level of inefficiency in UK manufacturing has either increased faster or fallen more slowly than

levels in other advanced economies. In other words there is
no evidence of increasing relative inefficiency. However, the
position is not that tests on the importance of increasing
inefficiency have proved negative but that no tests have in
fact been carried out. The obstacle to scientific testing is the
measurement problem referred to above. The claim that
productivity growth in UK industry has been retarded by a
higher level of efficiency has been made by Kilpatrick and
Lawson. Thus 'decentralized bargaining has constrained
productivity growth in the UK, compared with elsewhere. In
particular it has tended to lead to higher manning levels and
slower rates of adoption and diffusion than would otherwise
have been the case' (Kilpatrick and Lawson, 1980, p. 90).
The gist of the argument is that a more decentralized system
of bargaining has strengthened the power of workers and
enabled them to resist more successfully the adoption of new
industrial technology. The difficulty with this thesis is one of
evidence. The authors concede that 'the analysis does not
lend itself to statistical testing' (ibid., p. 90), and refer
instead to the results of a number of historical case studies
which are consistent with their analysis. It is very difficult,
however, to draw the authors' general conclusions about
international growth rates of productivity from a form of
evidence which is as limited as this. The overall conclusion to
be drawn from these arguments is that until firm evidence to
the contrary is provided very little weight if any should be
put on the argument that productivity growth in the UK has
been retarded by inefficiency.

Slow endogenous technical progress

The conclusion that the slow growth of productivity in UK
manufacturing is attributable to a slow rate of home-
produced technical progress emerges from the Verdoorn–
Kaldor hypothesis examined in chapter 2. There is no need
here to do anything more than restate the main findings of
investigations of the hypothesis which are

> (1) that in advanced economies a strong positive
> relationship exists between the growth rates of
> labour productivity and output in manufacturing

(but not between the growth rates of labour productivity and employment in manufacturing); and
(2) that this relationship represents endogenous
technical progress in the form of dynamic economies
of scale.

The cause of slow productivity growth is thus traced to a
slow rate of technical progress but this in turn is presented as
a consequence of a slow expansion of manufacturing rather
than a cause of it. The Verdoorn–Kaldor hypothesis is thus
another route to the conclusion that what appears to be a
cause of slow UK growth is more likely to be a symptom of
it.

The overall view of advocates of this position is that technical progress has been equally available to all, but more
fully exploited by those economies which have achieved
faster rates of manufacturing expansion. The claim that they
must obviously reject is that rates of technical progress are
autonomous; more precisely that differential rates of technical progress have been generated by something other than
the differential growth rates of output achieved and thus
have arisen exogenously amongst advanced economies.
Thus Kaldor puts the rhetorical question

> How can the progress of knowledge account for the fact that,
> for example, in the period 1954–1960 productivity in the Ger-
> man motor car industry increased at 7% per year and in Britain
> only 2.7% per year? Since large segments of the car industry in
> both countries were controlled by the same American firms,
> they must have had the same access to improvements in know-
> ledge and knowhow (Kaldor, 1966, p. 13).

And for Cripps and Tarling

> in groups of advanced countries . . . it is not unreasonable to
> suppose that all have access to much the same body of technical
> knowledge (Cripps and Tarling, 1973, p. 3).

Slow exogenous technical progress

The claim that technical progress has not been equally available to all is the message of Gomulka's (1971 and 1979)

alternative explanation of international differences in rates of productivity growth, and of the slow rate achieved in the UK. Gomulka's diffusion hypothesis is theorizing on a grand scale which presents a vast and sweeping view of the development of the nations of the world industrial economy, but within it there is a very specific explanation of slow growth in the UK. The argument starts with the proposition that five sources of technical progress are available to any economy:

(1) the domestic research and development (R and D) sector which produces innovations;
(2) the domestic non-R and D sector the expansion of which generates technical progress through dynamic economies of scale and learning by doing;
(3) capital goods imported from abroad embodying superior technology – 'embodied diffusion';
(4) imported licences and patents; and
(5) information from abroad provided by scientific journals, the exchange of personnel and so on – 'natural diffusion' – which in contrast to (3) and (4) is a foreign source which is virtually costless.

Although each of these five agents can contribute to technical progress a dominant agent will eventually emerge.

The development of a society towards an advanced industrial economy can be described in terms of a sequence of stages each of which is characterized by the dominant source of technical progress. In a traditional pre-industrial society the R and D sector will not exist and the limited extent of foreign trade and commerce will restrict the diffusion of technical progress from abroad. Learning-by-doing is the main carrier of the slow rate of technical progress experienced in the first stage of development. This gradual increase in productivity and output stimulates R and D activity and foreign trade and thus creates the conditions of the second take-off stage in which diffusion from abroad and domestic R and D activity become the main agents of technical progress. The third stage is one of sustained and full-scale industrial expansion. Growth is propelled by a rapidly expanding R and D sector and by diffusion from abroad, which is massively accelerated by the growing capacity of the economy to absorb and apply free innovations from elsewhere and to finance imports of machinery and patents through exports. However, this rapid expansion promotes the economy to the ranks of the world technological leaders. The economy is thus transformed from a diffusee of technical progress into a source of diffusion for others. The fourth stage is one in which the growth rate of productivity slackens as the benefits of diffusion are lost and the domestic R and D sector becomes the sole carrier of technical progress in the fully mature industrial economy.

This framework can be applied cross-sectionally to analyse differential rates of productivity growth within the group of advanced industrial economies. As described above the growth of labour productivity in the technologically most advanced economy is determined by the performance of its R and D sector. In other advanced economies the mechanism of productivity growth is more complex. Diffusion from the leader offers the potential of a faster rate of productivity growth, but a faster rate will only be realized if there is an adequate 'absorptive capacity'. This capacity will be enhanced by 'more receptive management attitudes, less worker resistance . . . and strong government institutions which assist in the technological transfer, especially the scientific effort and technical education' (Gomulka, 1979, p. 188). Thus the rate of diffusion enjoyed by an economy with a given export capacity is assumed to depend on

> (1) the gap between its own level of technology (T) and that of the most advanced economy (T^*) which Gomulka defines in relative terms as $(T^* - T)/T$; and
> (2) its absorptive capacity – a proxy for which is the technological level already achieved by the economy.

These assumptions imply a 'hat-shaped' relationship between rates of productivity growth (g_p) and relative technological gaps. An economy for which the technological gap is large will have a limited capacity to realize the high rate of productivity growth offered by diffusion, whereas an economy for which the gap is small will have a greater ability to realize a smaller potential. Since the rate of productivity growth

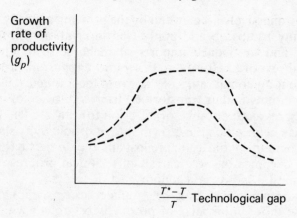

FIGURE 5.1   *The hat-shaped relationship*

generated by diffusion tends to be greater than that enjoyed by the leader, it is predicted that economies which exhibit an intermediate value of $(T^*-T)/T$ will exhibit the highest growth rates of productivity. This relationship is much more likely to take the form of a band rather than a single curve (figure 5.1) since T is not likely to be a very accurate proxy for the non-economic determinants of absorptive capacity. Economies at the same technological level may absorb technical progress through diffusion at different rates because of differences in social, cultural and institutional conditions. In this analysis the USA is identified as the technological leader. The superiority of US technology is inferred from the fact that over the post-war period (and before) the level of manufacturing output per man-hour has been much higher in the USA than elsewhere even though capital–output ratios in other economies have been the same or higher. This line of reasoning also provides a proxy measure of the technological gap since international differences in levels of technology will be proportional to international differences in levels of labour productivity provided that capital–output ratios are more or less the same in all countries. As this has in fact been the case the technological gap can be measured by the labour productivity gap. The prediction of this analysis for the very long run is that differences in productivity growth rates will disappear as all economies converge to the growth rate of the technological leader. However, persistent differences in the non-economic factors which determine absorptive capacity will result in productivity growth rates becoming equalized at different levels of productivity.

The Gomulka hypothesis offers a neat explanation of the two main features of the post-war productivity record of the UK shown in table 5.1 which are:

(1) the lower rate achieved in all periods compared to rates achieved elsewhere; and

(2) the improvement after the mid-1960s relative both to earlier achievements and to achievements in economies such as France and Germany.

Table 5.2 shows technological gaps in 1953 and 1965 as measured by the ratio of per capita GDP in the USA to per capita GDP in each economy.

At the beginning of the post-war period the technological gap between the UK and the USA was relatively small. Thus the growth of productivity available to the UK through dif-

Table 5.2
Technological gaps – ratio of US per capita GDP to national per capita GDP (measured at factor cost in 1958 US dollars)

	1953	1965
Austria	3.73	2.75
Belgium	2.13	2.01
Canada	1.41	1.41
Denmark	1.82	1.68
France	2.23	1.84
Germany	2.57	1.79
Italy	4.27	3.21
Japan	8.23	4.06
Netherlands	2.65	2.31
Norway	2.06	1.85
UK	1.96	1.98

Source: Gomulka (1971).

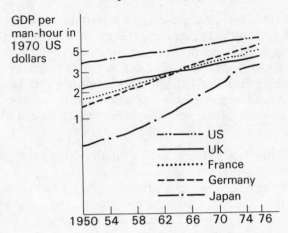

FIGURE 5.2   *Levels and growth rates of
productivity* (Source:
Maddison, 1979)

fusion was lower than that available in most other economies
and this is reflected in the comparative growth rates actually
achieved. By the mid-1960s, however, faster rates of
productivity had propelled several Western European
economies to technological levels close to that of the UK,
and in the late 1960s a technological gap had opened between these economies and the UK which pulled up productivity growth in the UK. This interaction between levels and
growth rates of productivity can be seen in figure 5.2 which
shows the record of the UK, the USA, Germany, France and
Japan in terms of GDP per man-hour. Productivity is measured vertically on a logarithmic scale which allows growth
rates to be represented by slopes.

The Gomulka hypothesis has been supported by a number
of formal tests on pooled time-series–cross-section data
including those of United Nations (1970), Cornwall (1976)
and Parikh (1978). A fairly typical formulation is that tested
by Cornwall (1977a, ch. 8):

$$g_m = a_0 + \frac{a_1}{q_r} + a_2 \frac{I}{Q_m} \qquad (5.11)$$

where g_m is the growth rate of manufacturing output – which shows the effect of but does directly measure the growth of productivity in manufacturing; q_r is the ratio of per capita income in the economy to per capita income in the USA, the inverse of which is the proxy measure of the technological gap; and I/Qm is the ratio of investment to output in manufacturing which is entered as a measure of the effort made to realize the benefits offered by diffusion. Cornwall's result for six large economies (USA, UK, France, Germany, Italy and Japan) for the period 1950–70 is:

$$g_m = -0.036 + \frac{0.953}{q_r} + 0.229 \frac{I}{Qm} \qquad R^2 = 0.80$$

$$(0.286) \quad (0.083) \qquad\qquad (5.12)$$

(standard errors are in parentheses). As would be expected from the information in figure 5.2 these results are sensitive to the exclusion of Japan from the sample.

Technical progress – endogenous or exogenous?

To sum up, we now have two apparently competing explanations of the slow rate of productivity growth in UK manufacturing: the Verdoorn–Kaldor argument is that the immediate cause has been the slow rate at which technical progress has been internally generated, which is traced back in turn to the slow expansion of manufacturing output. The Gomulka argument is that the immediate cause has been the slow rate at which technical progress has been diffused and absorbed into the UK from elsewhere, and this is a reflection of the high technological level of the post-war UK economy. In contrast to our examination of alternative hypotheses on labour and capital shortages we are here in the awkward position of finding empirical support of more or less equal strength for both of these explanations. There are several interpretations which can be put on this result. It is possible that the two hypotheses are not truly competitive in the sense that in post-war economies there may have been an interaction between the mechanisms described in each of them. In this case the empirical findings are what would be expected. However on two counts it is rather difficult to envisage the logic of an interaction which would allow the mechanisms of both hypotheses to operate at the same time. In the first place output growth tends to have opposite effects on productivity growth in the two systems: slower growth results in slower productivity growth in the Verdoorn–Kaldor system; but other things being equal slower growth will stimulate productivity growth in the Gomulka system by widening the technological gap. Secondly, the long-run outcome in the two systems is different: productivity growth rates converge in the Gomulka system whereas this is not the case in the Verdoorn–Kaldor system. Indeed, as will be clear from the next chapter, the Verdoorn–Kaldor hypothesis often appears as a key element in an explanation of divergent output and productivity trends in the long run. Another interpretation is that the Gomulka hypothesis describes the long long run whereas the Verdoorn–Kaldor hypothesis describes some divergent features of the adjustment path in the short long run. Finally it may be insisted that the hypotheses are fully competitive but that tests on them have not been formulated carefully enough to allow empirical evidence to discriminate between them. Although the first interpretation seems untenable it is not possible to say in the present state of knowledge whether the second or third interpretation is correct.

There are three conclusions to be drawn from the arguments reviewed in this chapter:

> (1) slow technical progress and not increasing inefficiency has been the main cause of slow productivity growth in the UK;
> (2) restrictions on both internal and external sources have been important in retarding technical progress in the UK; but
> (3) it is not possible to say that internal factors have been more or less important than external factors.

In particular, and in contrast to the case of the growth of the labour force and capital accumulation in UK manufacturing, the balance of evidence does not strongly favour the view that the slow growth of the resource of technical progress has been endogenous to the growth process.

6   Slow growth and trade performance

In the course of examining variants of the supply hypothesis on the causes of slow UK growth we have considered separately a number of arguments on the importance of demand factors and the evidence for them. A fully co-ordinated expression of the demand hypothesis is provided by the model of export-led growth, variants of which have been applied to the UK by a number of writers including Beckerman (1965, ch. 2), Kaldor (1978a) and Matthews (1973).

A model of trade performance and economic growth

What might be called the basic model consists of two elements:

> (1) a set of relationships between demand changes on the one hand and changes in factor supplies and productivity on the other; and
> (2) a 'fixed-price' model of adjustments in international trade.

The relationships between demand and resources involve induced increases in investment and technical progress and are those introduced in chapter 1 and described in more detail in sections of chapters 2, 4 and 5. The trade model is based on Harrod's (1933) application to the relationship between planned exports and imports of the multiplier mechanism which in Keynesian theory is applied to the relationship between planned savings and investment. The workings of the trade model are best understood by starting from first principles.

Consider a closed economy A which is self-sufficient in the production of all consumption and capital goods and in which all tax revenues are devoted to government expenditure and all savings (income not accounted for by consumption and taxation) are devoted to investment. These assumptions imply that the production of goods cannot be constrained by demand, for an increase in resources, the production of goods and income will generate a matching increase in demand through consumption, savings and taxation. Deficient demand and over-supply cannot exist. The expansion of output will thus be constrained only by the availability of the resources of labour, capital and technical progress. In short, Say's Law operates. This conclusion is not necessarily disturbed by the introduction of trade between economies. Think of *B* as another economy subject to the operation of Say's Law and suppose that *A* and *B* engage in trade. The fact that some income generated in *A* is now devoted to the purchase of goods produced in *B* (*B* goods) will not create over-supply in *A* if such purchases are matched by exports from *A*. In this case spending out of income generated in *A* on goods not produced in *A* will be covered by spending on *A* goods out of incomes not generated in *A*. Because *A*'s exports are *B*'s imports and vice-versa, if exports and imports are equal in *A* they are also equal in *B*. Thus if deficient demand does not exist in *A* excess demand does not exist in *B*. Suppose that from a position of trade balance residents of *B* for some reason decide to purchase less *A* goods and more *B* goods. The immediate result is that the total demand for *A* goods (*B* goods) will fall short of (exceed) production in *A* (*B*). *A* goods will suddenly be in excess supply and *B* goods will be in excess demand, which is another way of saying that a trade deficit will appear in *A* and a trade surplus in *B*. The effect of the deficient demand in *A* depends crucially on the form of the adjustment mechanism which now comes into operation.

Suppose that market and trade imbalances are corrected by induced changes in relative prices. In conditions of excess supply the price of *A* goods will fall in terms of *B* goods. This will (1) transfer real purchasing power from *A* to *B*; and (2) make *A* goods more attractive than *B* goods in both economies. Both of these effects will work in the same direction to stimulate the demand for exports from A and depress the demand for imports in A. The fall in the relative price of A goods will persist as long as A goods are in excess supply; and when the price of A goods has fallen to a market clearing level the adjustment to the initial disturbance will actually take place through a rise in net exports (exports minus imports) from A and a fall in net exports from B. The way in which these adjustments will actually come about depends on the prevailing institutional arrangements for international trade and payments. In a regime of fixed exchange rates the initial disturbance to the balance of trade will result in a fall in foreign currency reserves in A and a rise in reserves in B. As a consequence the domestic money supply and thus the domestic price level will fall in A and rise in B. If, however, the exchange rate is free to respond to market pressures, the excess supply of the currency of A (which is the counterpart of the excess supply of A goods) will force down its value against the currency of B. Exports from A will automatically become cheaper in B or more profitable to producers in A. Exactly the reverse will be the case for exports from B. In either regime the swifter are these adjustments the quicker will economy A (and B) return to the supply-determined path of expansion it would have followed had there been no disturbance to the balance of trade. In the limit the deficiency of demand in A (the excess demand in B) will be corrected instantaneously at unchanged levels of activity.

Markets may not work in the way just described, however. In highly competitive markets firms cannot influence prices and must accept changes in prices caused by variations in demand. Markets for traded commodities may not be highly competitive, however. In this case firms will be able to fix prices and respond to variations in demand by changing output and employment rather than prices. Furthermore it may be rational for firms to make adjustments in output rather than price if there is uncertainty about the duration of the demand change. Thus firms in A may respond to deficient demand by cutting production rather than prices, and those in B may respond to excess demand by expanding production rather than raising prices. There is some evidence that prices of manufactures are determined by movements in costs regardless of changes in pressure of demand, and that the typical response of a firm faced with an unanticipated fall in demand is to maintain prices but first to build up stocks and then to reduce output and employment.[1] Labour markets may also be uncompetitive. Trade unions in A may resort to wage inflation in an attempt to offset increases in the price of imports from B. The result of this will be general inflation, that is an increase in the price of A and B goods, rather than an increase in the relative price of B goods. The general result is that relative prices will not fluctuate to clear markets in non-competitive conditions. In this case induced changes in activity levels must be relied on to correct trade and market imbalances. Output in A will fall in the face of deficient demand and will rise in B in response to excess demand. These output changes will stimulate net exports from A and depress net exports from B and will persist until market and trade imbalances are eliminated. The government in A may attempt to speed up the adjustment process by running a budget surplus in order to reinforce the deflation. In the final outcome a market and trade equilibrium will be restored at a lower level of activity in A and a higher level in B. Thus in the 'fixed-price' model economy A is forced off the supply-determined path of expansion by deficient demand in the form of excessive imports. Say's Law does not hold and the expansion of output is demand constrained.[2] It is important to see that the cause of the contraction in A is excessive imports relative to exports in the *ex ante* sense. The effect of the contraction is to adjust actual imports to achieved exports. Thus in the observable outcome imports are not excessive.

In the 'fixed-price' model the expansion of output in A is governed by the growth of net exports from A, more precisely by the growth of foreign demand for its products relative to its propensity to import goods from abroad. This can be demonstrated in a simple way. In the absence of changes in relative prices the growth of imports in A and exports from A can be expressed as follows:

$$g_{ma} = g_a \cdot e_a \qquad (6.1)$$

$$g_{xa} = g_b \cdot e_b \qquad (6.2)$$

where g_{ma} is the growth rate of imports in A, g_a is the growth rate of output and income in A and e_a is the income elasticity of demand for imports in A, and where g_{xa} is the growth rate of exports from A, g_b is the growth rate of output and income in B and e_b is the income elasticity of demand for imports in B (for exports from A). The adjustment mechanism of the 'fixed-price' model steers economy A towards the position in which $g_{ma} = g_{xa}$, the condition of which is that

$$g_a = \frac{e_b \cdot g_b}{e_a} \qquad (6.3)$$

Equation (6.3) says that the growth rate of output in A is limited to the growth rate of exports from A divided by the income elasticity of demand for imports in A, or, equivalently, that the ratio of growth rates in A and B is given by the ratio of the income elasticity of demand for imports in B and A. An attempt by the government in A to increase the growth rate of output above $(e_b \cdot g_b)/e_a$ by running a budget deficit would result in a growing trade deficit which could not be sustained in the long run. A growth rate below $(e_b \cdot g_b)/e_a$ could be sustained by the use of a growing budget surplus the counterpart of which would be a growing trade surplus.

Now think of B not as one trading partner but as the rest of the world (many other economies). This modification does not disturb the result demonstrated in the previous paragraph but does have implications for the pattern of international trade. The initial disturbance will now take the form of a trade deficit in A matched by a trade surplus spread across many other economies. The expansion of income in many other economies will stimulate trade between them with the result that, compared to the two-country model, a smaller proportion of the income growth abroad which accompanies A's deficit will be spent on A's exports. As a consequence the process of adjustment in A will involve a smaller rise in exports and therefore a larger fall in imports. The overall result in the 'fixed-price' model with many economies is that trade will tend to become concentrated in other economies: A's share of total world exports and total world imports will tend to fall.

The model of a demand constrained economy is presented above as the case of extreme price rigidity, to be contrasted with the case in which complete price flexibility ensures that the economy steers itself along a path of expansion limited only by the supply of resources. This stark contrast makes the exposition easier but conceals intermediate cases. The adjustment to trade and market imbalances may take the form of sluggish movements in relative prices together with less pronounced changes in activity levels. The claim of the demand hypothesis in this case is that adjustments operate mainly through variations in income and output and not through variations in relative prices.

The 'fixed-price' model describes a demand constraint on the expansion of actual output. A progressive relationship between demand, trade performance and the expansion of potential output (economic growth) is established by extending the trade adjustment model to include the relationships between demand, actual output and potential output referred to in the opening section of this chapter. Thus the initial contraction of demand and output in A will depress investment and retard technical progress. Different writers have given different degress of emphasis to these relationships. Thus Beckerman (1965, ch. 2) emphasizes the link between trade performance, investment expectations and technical progress embodied in new capital goods, whereas Thirwall (1980, ch. 11) emphasizes the link between trade performance, output growth and technical progress in the form of dynamic economies of scale. The various demand effects which retard growth in A and stimulate growth elsewhere are likely to become self-reinforcing. The decline in investment and technical progress caused by an exogenous contraction in the demand for A goods will tend to make them less attractive in terms of design and quality in both domestic and foreign markets. A will thus suffer an induced contraction in net exports and demand which will further reduce the growth of potential output, and so on. In other words the initial exogenous contraction in demand will give rise to a sequence of endogenous contractions in demand and growth. Forces of cumulative causation will thus act on the initial disturbance so as to lock economy A into a vicious circle of falling growth and falling net exports. Other economies will experience this process in reverse.

It is important to see that the trade–demand hypothesis on the causes of economic growth is (or should be) saying something more than that the growth process is cumulative and circular. To say that demand creates supply and supply creates demand is to say everything and nothing about growth, and in particular is to eliminate all other explanations by simply swallowing them. The distinctive claim of the trade–demand hypothesis is that the demand changes are the prime mover in the growth process and that the relationship from demand growth to the growth of resources and supply is more regular, more powerful and more systematic than the reverse. An implication of this is that the relationship between trade performance and economic growth will be self-reinforcing only to a moderate degree. Thus the decline of economy A will not be cumulative and other economies will not expand without limit. In A's case the visible signs of the operation of the trade–demand mechanisms will be a conjunction of (1) comparatively slow growth, (2) a falling share of world exports and (3) rising import penetration. In terms of equation (6.3) the outcome would be one in which the ratio of g_a to g_b (and e_b to e_a) fell towards a more or less constant value less than one.

Suitably qualified, the trade–demand model can be used to analyse the expansion of a sector within a trading economy. Under the assumptions of the model the growth of manufacturing output in A will depend on two factors:

> (1) positively on the growth of the exogenous component of demand for the manufactures of A and
> (2) negatively on the propensity in A to import manufactured goods.

Imports come from the manufacturing sectors of other economies and for an open economy the relevant component of demand will be that exercised by foreigners. Thus the expansion of the manufacturing sector depends on trade performance in manufacturing; but there may be a degree of freedom at the sectoral level which is not available at the national level. A rate of manufacturing expansion faster than that set by (1) and (2) would result in a growing trade deficit in manufactures, but this could be sustained if it were offset by a growing surplus in non-manufactures. Whether faster growth is possible depends on the structure of the economy's balance of payments and on the scope for a sustained expansion in net exports of non-manufactures. In an economy resembling that of the UK in the post-war period the main candidate for the provider of compensation would be the invisible account, or rather the account in private services which, unlike other invisible items such as interest, profits and dividends can make an additional contribution to the balance of payments without a prior net outflow. For such an economy the value of exports of private services would not be more than half that of manufactures but would account for a relatively large share of a relatively small world market (in the case of the UK, 26 per cent in 1955 falling to 16 per cent in 1973).[3] This means that both the base and scope for an increase in net exports of private services would be too small to allow the manufacturing sector to expand in the long run at a rate significantly greater than that allowed by its own trade performance.

We are now in a position to identify an explanation of slow UK growth. The claim of the trade–demand model (supplements with the key sector hypothesis) is that the cause of slow growth has been a demand constraint on manufacturing imposed by an inferior growth rate of net exports and manifest in rising import penetration and a falling share of world exports. The retort to all arguments about the importance of supply factors is that slow productivity growth, poor investment performance, a slow expansion of employment and slow output growth have been associated together in the UK only as joint products of poor trade performance, and not as causes and effect.

UK trade performance

The success of the UK manufacturing sector in resisting foreign competition in foreign markets can be measured by

Table 6.1
Percentage shares in the value of world exports of manufactures, 1950–75

	1950	1960	1965	1970	1975
UK	25.5	16.5	13.9	10.8	9.3
France	9.9	9.6	8.8	8.7	10.2
Germany	7.3	19.3	19.1	19.8	20.3
Italy	26.6	5.1	6.7	7.2	7.5
Others		21.0	21.8	23.3	21.4
Japan	3.4	6.9	9.4	11.7	13.6
USA	27.3	21.6	20.3	18.5	17.7

Source: Brown and Sheriff (1979). The world is defined as the countries covered in the table. 'Others' are Canada, Sweden, Switzerland and the Benelux countries.

the UK share of total manufacturing exports. Table 6.1 shows a steady deterioration in UK performance and the very marked contrast between this record and that of other advanced economies. The resistance offered to foreign competition in domestic markets can be measured in a number of ways. Table 6.2 shows a steady and substantial increase in import penetration as measured by the ratio of manufactured imports to total domestic sales of manufactures (the latter measured by domestic production plus imports minus exports). A difficulty with this measure is that other things being equal import penetration is shown to increase as exports increase. However the use of other measures which do not have this property (such as the ratio of imports to total domestic production) does not alter the general picture. The attention of some commentators has been caught

Table 6.2
The penetration of manufactured imports in the UK, 1955–73 (percentages)

1955	6.0	1970	13.0
1960	8.0	1973	18.0
1965	9.0		

Source: Brown and Sheriff (1979). Penetration is measured by imports divided by total domestic production plus imports minus exports.

by the fact that the increase in import penetration in UK
manufacturing has been more or less matched by an increase
in the ratio of UK manufactured exports to domestic sales.
However, it is incorrect to suggest as some do that this outcome refutes the trade–demand hypothesis. Indeed if anything the reverse is the case, for the adjustment mechanism
of the model ensures that imports equal exports *ex post*.
Thus the predicted outcome of the model is that imports and
exports (each expressed as a proportion of domestic sales or
of any other single magnitude) will move together. The evidence on UK trade performance is broadly consistent with
the trade–demand hypothesis but an inspection of summary
trends hardly constitutes a rigorous test of it. We can take
the assessment one stage further by asking what have been
the causes of the trends shown in tables 6.1 and 6.2.

A priori considerations suggest the fall in the UK share of
manufactured exports is a result of one or more of the following factors:

(1) a decline in the competitiveness of UK exports
in terms of price;
(2) a decline in the competitiveness of UK exports
in terms of non-price characteristics;
(3) 'trade bias' in the form of a concentration of
exports in slowly growing markets, or in products the
demand for which is slowly growing; and
(4) a constraint on the capacity of domestic producers to supply exports.

We can expect any one of the following factors to cause an
increase in import penetration:

(1) a decline in the price competitiveness of import
substitutes produced in the UK;
(2) a decline in the non-price competitiveness of
import substitutes; and
(3) a constraint on the capacity of domestic producers to supply import substitutes.

It should be clear from the previous section that an explanation in which changes in price competitiveness and capacity
effects were important would be inconsistent with the

trade–demand hypothesis. A key assumption of the trade–demand model is that changes in relative prices are not an important influence on trade flows. The main conclusion of the model is that capacity depends on trade performance rather than the reverse. Thus if we find that price and capacity effects are relatively unimportant we can have more confidence in the trade–demand hypothesis, and of course vice-versa.

Price competitiveness

The many difficulties involved in measuring international price competitiveness are very clearly set out in HM Treasury (1978) and at greater length in Enoch (1978). The choice of measures depends on the degree of competition in international markets. If markets are imperfectly competitive a measure appropriate for an analysis of the UK export share is the ratio of the prices of UK exports of manufactures to a weighted average of competitors' export prices. An increase in the ratio indicates a deterioration in price competitiveness. An appropriate measure for an analysis of import penetration is the ratio of the UK price of manufactures to a weighted average of the prices of manufactured imports. Both measures are expressed in a common currency to capture the effects of changing exchange rates. There will be very little movement in relative prices, however, if international markets are either perfectly competitive or oligopolistic. In either case a measure of the ratio of units costs is more appropriate and has the additional advantage of displaying in a single index the relative cost and profitability of producing both exports and import substitutes.

Although there is no comprehensive study of UK trade performance and price competitiveness in the post-war period the results of a number of more limited investigations do not provide evidence of either a systematic positive relationship between price competitiveness and the UK export share or a systematic negative relationship between price competitiveness and import penetration in the UK. Kaldor (1978b) shows that between 1956 and 1975 the UK share of manufactured exports from the major advanced market economies fell steadily from 18.7 to 9.3 per cent during which period price competitiveness (measured by the ratio of UK unit labour costs to unit labour costs elsewhere) first deteriorated by 10 per cent (rising from an index value of 100 in 1956 to 110 in 1960) and then improved by 8 per cent (falling from 110 in 1960 to 101 in 1975). The positive relationship between movements in price competitiveness and the export share in the 1950s and early 1960s is confirmed by evidence provided by Krause (1968, tables 5.3 and 5.6) for the period 1954–66, and by Junz and Rhomberg (1965, table 3) for the period 1953–63. However, the negative relationship for the later period is confirmed by evidence cited by Brown and Sheriff (1979, table 10.16) which shows the UK share of world exports of manufactures to have fallen from 13.4 per cent in 1966 to 9.4 per cent in 1973 while competitiveness measured by a composite index improved steadily by about 10 per cent (falling from an index value of 107.2 in 1966 to a value of 96.0 in 1973, with 1970 = 100).

Investigations of price competitiveness and import penetration in the UK are less numerous but more disappointing for theoretical expectations. Thus Krause's evidence (1968, tables 5.10 and 5.11) for the period 1956–64 shows a steady rise in import penetration in UK manufacturing accompanied by a more or less constant index of price competitiveness. Panić's investigation of import penetration in the UK between 1957 and 1972 points to 'the relative insignificance of changes in prices' (Panić, 1975, p. 5). And an OECD investigation (1980, pp. 21–26) of the period since 1965 shows an improvement in the competitiveness of UK manufactures in terms of price and unit labour costs accompanied by a steady rise in import penetration.

Thus, with the exception of the behaviour of the export share in the 1950s and early 1960s, there is no sign of the expected relationships between price competitiveness, the export share and import penetration. It should not be concluded from this that movements in relative prices have had no effect whatsoever on UK trade performance. It would be surprising if this were so given the empirical evidence for the UK that levels of imports and exports are sensitive to

changes in price competitiveness (estimates of long-run
export price elasticities are typically between −1.5 and
−2.0, and estimates of import price elasticities typically
between −0.2 and −1.5).[4] What can be said is that the
effects of changes in relative prices appear to have been
overridden by other more powerful factors acting at the
same time.

Capacity constraints

The basic argument on capacity constraints and trade performance is that an increase in the internal pressure of
demand on capacity will

> (1) divert production from export sales to home
> sales (thus reducing the export share); and
> (2) as bottlenecks appear in domestic production,
> induce more imports (thus increasing import pene-
> tration).

From this argument we should expect that capacity effects
will be generated by short-run fluctuations of demand over
the cycle, and that the effects will be greater the greater and
faster is the change in demand over the cycle. There is evidence that this is so. An early study by Ball, Eaton and
Steuer (1966) for the period 1954–66 shows that fluctuations in the UK export share in manufactures about the
trend are inversely related to the internal pressure of
demand. A disaggregated study of the period 1963–74 by
Hughes and Thirwall (1977) shows that in 21 UK manufacturing industries the movement about the trend of the ratio
of imports to domestic production is closely related to the
pressure of demand for labour. Hughes and Thirwall's findings are confirmed by Eltis's (1979b) demonstration that
industrial import penetration of the UK market advanced
most rapidly in 1963–64, 1967–68 and 1972–74 when rapid
expansion encountered supply bottlenecks.

It is difficult to say whether or not these results make out a
case against the claim that trade performance governs the
growth of capacity over the long run. The argument that
they do not is simply that evidence of capacity effects on
movements of trade performance about the trend tell us

nothing about the trend, long-run, relationship between trade performance and capacity. On the other hand the distinction between the cycle and the trend becomes blurred if a ratchet mechanism operates. Thus, if the fall in the export share (the rise in import penetration) when demand rises is greater than the rise in the export share (the fall in import penetration) when demand falls, cyclical effects will become absorbed into the trend. Smyth (1968) and Hughes and Thirwall (1977) provide some evidence for the UK that cyclical movements in the export share and the import ratio have been subject to a ratchet effect. However, it is not easy to see that such effects can account for much of the observed difference between the trade performance of the UK and that of other economies. The problem is simply that over much of the post-war period economies whose trade performance was superior to that of the UK experienced margins of spare capacity which were either less than that experienced in the UK (in the case of France and Germany) or roughtly equal to it (in the case of Italy, Japan and the US).[5]

Trade bias

The relationship between UK export performance and the product and market structure of UK exports has been thoroughly investigated by a number of writers including Major (1968) for the period 1954–66, Panić and Seward (1966) for the period 1959–64, and Panić and Rajan (1979) for the period 1955–73. The conclusion which all studies reach is that the unfavourable trend in UK export performance is not attributable to trade bias in either form. The UK does less well than other economies in selling what are broadly the same goods in the same markets.

Non-price competitiveness

If the importance of other factors is found to be either small or negligible we arrive by a process of elimination at the conclusion that the dominant cause of poor UK trade performance has been a worsening of non-price competitiveness. Many economists subscribe to this view; but they do so uneasily for the cause which it seems must be important is not particularly well-defined and there has been no full empirical demonstration of its effects. The non-price ingredients of competitiveness are usually thought of as including marketing effort, delivery time, design, reliability, ease of maintenance and after-sales service. Much of what passes for positive evidence on their importance consists of the anecdotes and impressions of businessmen, finance ministers and the chairmen of public bodies. A notable attempt to provide more comprehensive evidence of a quantitative kind is the work of the UK National Economic Development Office reported in Connell (1979, ch. 3). This shows that for product ranges in which the scope for non-price competitiveness is large (that is for technologically sophisticated goods such as machine tools) both the level and growth of the value per metric ton of UK exports has since the early 1960s been lower than that of the exports of more successful trading economies such as France and Germany. The inference drawn from this finding is that the low value of UK exports reflects inferior product quality rather than lower costs and prices for the same standard of product. More familiar measures which are sensitive to changes in the non-price competitiveness of tradable UK goods are the income elasticities of demand for UK imports and exports. Estimates of the UK income elasticity of demand for manufactured imports range from 2.61 (Taplin, 1973) for the period 1953/4–1969/70 to 3.09 (Panić, 1975) for the period 1957–72. These figures are roughly 50 per cent higher than estimates for other advanced economies (apart from the USA). They are also substantially higher than estimates for the same period of the world income elasticity of demand for UK manufactured exports, which are close to unity; see Houthakker and Magee (1969) for the period 1951–66 and Thirwall (1980, ch. 9) for the period 1963–74. These estimates in turn are much lower than those for other advanced economies (again apart from the USA) whose exports are more sensitive to changes in world income by a factor of 2 or 3.

In order fully to illustrate the failure of the UK to produce manufactured goods of the quality and design required to capture markets it is necessary to consider almost every heading of the Standard Industrial Classification. The picture is one of the unrelenting success of foreign producers both in product ranges such as consumer durables, motor cycles and office machinery in which the UK was once well established, and in new industries such as microelectronics in which the UK has failed to establish itself. The exceptions to this record, such as the food-processing industry and parts of the chemical industry, are very few. The underlying causes of this failure to maintain quality in new and existing products have not been much researched and are not well understood, but the torpor of UK manufacturing is in some part a result of the slowness of its expansion.

The theory and the facts

What degree of support does the empirical evidence on UK trade performance give to the trade–demand hypothesis? The statistical series and studies reviewed in the previous section were not designed as, and do not provide a formal test of, the hypothesis, but the circumstantial evidence they offer is not at all unkind to it. The conjunction of slow growth, rising import penetration and a falling export share is an outcome which the hypothesis evisages; and an examination of the causes of the trends in UK trade performance does not reveal that factors which the hypothesis must assume to be unimportant have in fact been important. The UK has not been significantly disadvantaged either by the price of its products or by capacity constraints (or by trade bias). The problem has been one of product quality broadly defined. While other economies have produced high-value, high-quality manufactures, the UK has struggled with a low-quality product range which has been unattractive to purchasers both at home and abroad. To express the problem in this way, however, raises the question of whether at the end of the day the trade–demand hypothesis is not really a supply hypothesis in disguise. Has not the problem of demand been that the selection of goods offered has not attracted buyers? There are two points to make on this. First, the conventional supply hypothesis (that outlined in chapter 1) must be substantially redefined if it is to accommodate the trade–demand hypothesis in this way, for the identified constraint derives not from the unavailability of resources but from the inefficient employment of available resources in the production of goods that no-one wants. Secondly, it follows from this that any modifications to the trade–demand hypothesis should not be in the direction of a neo-classical formulation of the supply hypothesis, the central claim of which is that the market allocates available resources so as to provide a level and pattern of output which most satisfies existing tastes and which cannot be bettered without an increase in the supply of resources.

Some objections

It is possible to accept completely the empirical evidence on UK growth and trade performance but to put on it an interpretation very different from that suggested in the previous section. The general view on which conflicting interpretations are based is that changes in the balance of resource use between the sectors of a trading economy are the sign of an adjustment to changing conditions in world markets which is both normal and desirable. A relative expansion of some sectors of a trading economy (and thus inevitably a relative decline in others) is the means by which gains from international specialization are realized. Thus, far from being a disorder causing slow growth, a trade-induced decline in a sector is a means to increased efficiency and expansion which only a misguided government would seek to prevent. The implication of this 'market adjustment' view for the analysis of UK growth is that slow growth has been caused by something other than the declining share of UK manufactures in world markets, and indeed that any attempt to arrest this decline would have made matters worse.

A formulation of this view concerned with very recent developments is the argument of Forsyth and Kay (1980) on de-industrialization and North Sea oil. The authors' claim is that a decline in UK manufacturing will be

(1) essential if the resources provided by North Sea oil are to yield benefits in the form of increased consumption; and
(2) inevitable provided that the government takes no active steps to prevent it.

The instrument of change is the oil-induced rise in the exchange rate, the effect of which will be to reduce the relative (and possibly absolute) size of the UK manufacturing sector by reducing exports and increasing imports. Resources are thereby squeezed out of the domestic manufacturing sector and made available for the production of non-tradable commodities such as housing and services which the community wants but which it cannot obtain by way of a direct trade exchange for oil. In other words the rise in the exchange rate is the means by which oil is exchanged for foreign manufactures and domestic manufactures are exchanged for domestic non-tradable goods and services. The decline in domestic manufacturing is simply a part of this conversion process. This is an analysis of the very recent history and prospects of the UK which has nothing to say about the significance of the trade performance of the UK manufacturing sector during the period before 1976. The argument is relevant to the question of the extent to which UK manufacturing should be expanded to increase growth in the future, and we shall return to it in this context in the next chapter.

A formulation which is relevant to the historical period is Harrod's retort that

> the reference to [the declining share of Britain in world exports of manufactures] as evidence of decline is surely one of the most absurd ever perpetrated in a diagnosis. The British share of world exports has declined, is declining and will continue to decline, hopefully at an accelerated pace . . . the reason why our 'share' in world exports of manufactures has declined is that our 'share' of manufacturing population in the world has greatly declined. The main gainers against us . . . have been the Italians and the Japanese, who have been pulling a big proportion of their population out of agriculture into industry (Harrod, 1967, pp. 507–8).

It may be that the fall in the UK share of world manufacturing exports is at least in part a result of an increase in the size of the denominator caused by the emergence of new producers; but this argument does not explain the rise in the ratio of manufactured imports to UK production. The fact that there are more foreign producers does not explain why purchasers in the UK have increasingly preferred foreign products. If UK manufacturers have become less competitive than foreign manufactures in UK markets it is difficult to argue that they have not also become less competitive in foreign markets. Thus it is probably an overstatement to argue that the fall in the UK export share is entirely attributable to the emergence of new producers. Indeed the degree of overstatement involved may be quite large. Between 1956 and 1974 the UK share of manufacturing employment in the major developed market economies fell by about 30 per cent; but the fall in the UK share of manufactured exports from the same economies over the same period was about 50 per cent. The percentage increases in the Italian and Japanese export shares over this period (114 and 157 per cent respectively) were very much larger than the percentage increases in their employment shares (18 and 53 per cent respectively). On the other hand France (by 36 per cent) and Germany (by 30 per cent) managed to increase their export shares over this period with virtually no increase in their employment shares.[6] The argument that changes in the international pattern of manufacturing exports are no more than a reflection of changes in the international pattern of manufacturing employment is thus unconvincing. This is not to deny that the changing pattern of employment has had some effect and that normal market adjustments have occurred; but the claim of the trade–demand hypothesis is not that any loss of world markets is pathological – rather that a loss substantially greater than that which changing world conditions require of other economies will cause relatively slow growth.

Notes

1. For evidence on industrial pricing in the UK see Coutts, Godley and Nordhaus (1978).
2. The objection to Say's Law examined in this chapter is essentially that a system of labour and commodity markets will not be self-regulating at full employment if imperfections exist. This argument should be distinguished from the question of whether a stable full employment equilibrium can be said to

exist in a theoretical sense. For a short account of both objections which shows the importance of the 'fixed-price' 'flexible-price' issue in another area see Hahn and Neild (1980). See also Minford (1980).

3. For detailed evidence on the potential contribution of services to the UK balance of payments see Sargent (1979), Brown and Sheriff (1979, pp. 245–6) and Singh (1977, pp. 120–1).

4. For a survey of estimates of price elasticities for UK imports and exports see Thirwall (1980, pp. 210–12 and 231–9).

5. For estimates of capacity utilization in seven advanced economies over the period 1960–76 see Manison (1978, table 16).

6. Changes in export shares are calculated from Brown and Sheriff (1979, table 10.5 and chart 10.3), and changes in employment shares are calculated from OECD (1961, 1969 and 1976).

7 Recent history and current policy

The task that remains is to see what the analysis of the previous chapters implies about the direction and components of a growth policy, and to compare such a policy with what is currently being done. It is important to be clear about the sort of policy conclusions it is possible to draw from the analysis of the previous chapters. An explanation of why UK growth has not matched that achieved elsewhere will not provide us with a detailed inventory of the measures that could be taken to improve growth; still less will it supply estimates of the magnitude of the adjustments that would be required to achieve any increase in growth thought desirable. What it can do at most is to indicate the direction in which a growth policy should proceed and to suggest the basic components of such a policy. Before we look at these issues it is useful briefly to recap on the argument so far, and essential to say something about UK growth in the period since 1973.

The argument so far

The position we have now reached can be summarised as follows.

(1) The suggestion that economic theory has little or nothing to say about the causes of growth is false. It is true that there is no agreed theory of the causes of growth but there are competing explanations which are reasonably well defined. The neo-classical theory that a market economy tends to a self-regulating path of full employment growth

attributes differences in growth to differences in the exogen-ousiy given supply of factor inputs and productivity. In contrast the Keynesian theory that a market economy does not regulate itself in this way indicates that in the final analysis economic growth depends on the growth of demand which is exogenous to the system. Differences in growth rates are thus attributable to the differing degrees of success with which economies have attracted external demand for their products. Both theories agree that growth will be increased by improvements in the efficiency with which existing resources are used.

(2) The immediate cause of slow growth in the UK has been the slow expansion of the UK manufacturing sector. The argument that the UK has suffered from the overexpan-sion of the non-market sector is difficult to make theoreti-cally and is not supported by international comparisons or by evidence for the UK.

(3) The supply of labour and capital has not been an exogenous constraint on the expansion of UK manufactur-ing. On the contrary the supply of labour and capital has been strongly influenced by the expansion of manufacturing output actually achieved, which implies that more labour and capital would have been forthcoming if other constraints had been less binding.

(4) Productivity growth in UK manufacturing has been restricted by a supply of exogenous technical progress which has been less abundant than that enjoyed by the manufactur-ing sectors of many other advanced economies. However, home-grown technical progress has also been retarded by the slow expansion of manufacturing output actually achieved.

(5) Productivity growth in UK manufacturing has not been retarded by increasing inefficiency in the form of increasing overmanning and underproduction. Productivity growth may have been depressed by the higher level of inefficiency in UK manufacturing but this effect has not been demonstrated theoretically or empirically.

(6) The most binding constraint on the expansion of overall economic activity in the UK has been the weakness of the demand for UK manufactures in world markets. This

has been due to worsening non-price competitiveness. Had the demand for UK manufactures been stronger than it was, faster economic growth would not have been prevented by limitations in the supply of labour and capital, and would not have been substantially impeded by the available supply of technical progress.

Conclusions (2) to (6) have been stated categorically to avoid a tedious repetition of the qualification that they are based on available evidence which in some cases is less than abundant. They should, however, be read with this in mind.

Recent history

Since 1973 the UK economy has suffered from a worsening of existing trends in trade performance and from a set of depressive impulses which have been felt in all advanced economies and which were by and large absent from the earlier period. The result was that in 1974, after a long period of comparatively slow growth, the UK economy entered a phase of virtual stagnation and now faces a period of absolute decline.

The UK share of world manufactured exports has been maintained since 1973 at about 9 per cent; but import penetration in UK manufacturing has soared from 18 per cent in 1973 to just over 25 per cent in 1979. The deterioration in trade in manufactures has more than cancelled out the improvement in the trade balance in fuels due to the discovery of North Sea oil and gas. In 1980 the UK has become approximately self-sufficient in oil, but the effect of this has been only to moderate the trade-induced decline and not to halt or reverse it. Since the early 1970s governments in all advanced economies have come to hold the conviction that the price that has to be paid for full employment in terms of inflation has risen very substantially, and have promoted the control of inflation above all other objectives. As a result all governments have introduced deflationary policies of varying degrees of severity in an attempt to substitute more unemployment for less inflation. There is not much agreement about the underlying factors which have provoked the worldwide response. One immediate cause has been the ten-fold increase in the price of OPEC oil between 1973/74 and 1979. This has both acted as a deflationary tax on oil-importing economies and provoked deflationary policies aimed at suppressing secondary wage and price increases. Other factors which may have been important include the emergence of strong inflationary expectations, and the volatile movements in exchange rates following the breakdown of the Bretton Woods system of fixed exchange rates in 1971 which have made governments more reluctant to embark on reflationary policies which incur balance of payments deficits.[1]

Under the combined effects of these factors growth in the UK and other advanced economies during the 1970s has been retarded to rates substantially below those achieved earlier. The magnitudes involved are shown in table 7.1. The UK economy is now being propelled into an absolute economic decline by a chronic deterioration in trade competitiveness exacerbated by the combined effects of a world

Table 7.1
Annual rates of growth of GDP and GDP per man-hour at constant prices, 1951–73 and from 1973 (percentages)

	GDP		GDP/MH	
	1951–73	1973–79	1951–73	1973–78
Belgium	4.1	2.4	4.5	4.3
Canada	5.1	3.3	3.1	1.4
Denmark	3.9	1.8	4.0	1.3
France	5.1	2.9	4.9	3.9
Germany	5.9	2.3	5.8	4.2
Italy	5.2	2.3	5.3	4.1
Japan	9.5	4.0	7.5	3.9
Netherlands	5.0	2.5	4.1	3.4
Norway	4.2	4.3	4.4	4.0
Sweden	3.8	1.6	3.8	1.4
UK	2.8	0.8	2.8	2.0
USA	3.5	2.3	2.3	1.1

Source: As for table 1.1 for 1951–73; for the period after 1973, Maddison (1980).

recession and domestic deflation. During 1980 UK GDP fell by $4\frac{1}{2}$ per cent, manufacturing output fell by $11\frac{1}{2}$ per cent, and unemployment rose to just over 2 million. The consensus amongst half a dozen reputable forecasting bodies is that if policies and all other relevant circumstances remain unchanged this collapse will progress to produce 3 million unemployed in 1982 and a slump more severe than that experienced in the worst years of the Great Depression.

Current policy

Although the present Conservative Government came to power in 1979 with the belief that all previous administrations had misdirected the economy, its strategy for growth is in large part a development of policies first introduced by the previous Labour administration in the wake of Mr Callaghan's declaration in 1976 that 'we can no longer spend our way out of a recession'. Present policies have been interpreted in some political circles as the expression of a deranged system of thought. This is a complete misconception which impedes any serious assessment of them. The Conservative strategy is a direct and entirely coherent application of the neo-classical supply hypothesis of growth. The underlying view is that if the structure of the economy were to resemble the model of perfect competition there would be neither the need nor scope for a government policy to promote growth. Allied to this is the conviction that even though perfect competition does not prevail it is not within the powers of a government to bring about a sustainable increase in the rate of economic growth. Thus, the most that a government can and should do about growth is to remove obstacles to efficiency and competition and thereby create the conditions in which a spontaneous and sustainable increase in growth can occur. The case for this strategy of *laissez faire* has been largely made out on *a priori* grounds without detailed reference to evidence.

The identified obstacles to growth are inflation and a set of institutional and fiscal barriers to the flexible and efficient working of the market economy. The argument on inflation and growth has not been very clearly spelt out. The general idea seems to be

> (1) that high and varying rates of inflation create
> uncertainty which makes it difficult for businessmen
> to plan efficiently;
> (2) that a high inflation rate requires that resources
> which could be more productively used elsewhere be
> devoted to the dissemination of information about
> price changes and to the rearrangement of trading
> activities; and
> (3) that the higher interest rates required to com-
> pensate lenders for higher inflation will retard
> investment.

The specific argument on market imperfections is simply
that through spontaneous increases in efficiency the liberal-
ized economy will naturally expand to realise the potential
provided by resources. The instruments of the policy are:

> (1) a progressive fiscal and monetary deflation
> designed to reduce inflation; and
> (2) a wide range of measures designed to promote
> efficiency and competition.

Thus there are commitments to amend the legal position of
trade unions, to abolish price and dividend controls, to create inner-city enterprise zones, to strengthen anti-monopoly
legislation, to denationalize, to refrain from intervening in
wage fixing in the private sector, to refrain from supporting
lame ducks and, most notably, to reduce the burden of
income tax substantially. The Government's aim is to reduce
the basic rate of income tax to a maximum of 25 per cent. At
the time of writing the basic rate had been cut from 33 to 30
per cent, and the highest rate on earned income reduced
from 83 to 60 per cent.[2] It is somewhat out of keeping with
the Government's view of the nature of the economy and
policy to describe its strategy in the conventional terms of
targets and instruments. The Government seems to expect
as much from the general shift in attitudes which it hopes its
policies will create as it expects from direct economic relationships between the changes it has made and economic
growth.

Will current policy work?

Does the explanation of UK growth summarized at the beginning of this chapter suggest that this policy is well-directed? To answer this question we must look a little more closely at the mechanisms on which the policy depends. The Conservative strategy is by design crucially dependent on the operation of neo-classical mechanisms. This can be seen most clearly in respect of the fiscal and monetary deflation. Neo-classical mechanisms are being relied on to convert the deflation of demand into lower rates of inflation at levels of activity which are depressed only temporarily and by a small amount. The transition to conditions of lower inflation favourable to growth is thus relatively quick and painless; but the less the economy works like a neo-classical system the greater will be the impact of the deflation on employment and output, and the less will be the impact on the inflation rate. Such an outcome would constitute a very serious threat to the Conservative strategy on two counts. In the first place it would make it very difficult for the Government to make a significant additional reduction in tax rates. The anti-inflation policy requires a progressive reduction in the surplus of public expenditure over tax revenue; but reduced output and higher unemployment causes public expenditure to rise as the cost of supporting the unemployed grows and as nationalized industries make larger losses or small profits, and causes tax revenue to fall as the tax base contracts. Thus there is an adverse effect on the borrowing requirement of the public sector which is solely due to the slump. In this situation a government committed to pre-set fiscal and monetary targets will find that there is no scope for cuts in taxation and may indeed be forced to raise taxes. The effect of the slump on the budget means that the Government can cut taxes or retain its fiscal and monetary targets but that it will be unlikely to be able to do both. The firmness of the Conservative commitment to deflation means that in this case further tax cuts will be sacrificed. The other problem is simply that the greater are the output and employment effects of the deflation the greater will be the damage to productive capacity and growth inflicted by the induced

slump in investment and by the adverse effect of the recession on the growth of productivity. Thus if neo-classical
mechanisms do not work the Conservative strategy will have
to rely on the effects of institutional reforms (but not more
tax cuts) and a slowly falling inflation rate being sufficiently
powerful to (1) counteract the perverse effects of the policy
itself and (2) lift the economy out of the trade-induced
recession from which it is also suffering.

We can now return to the evidence. A central message of
the analysis summarized at the beginning of this chapter is
that in its generation of growth the UK economy has not
behaved like a neo-classical system. The factors which have
been most powerful in governing growth have been those
that would not be important in a neo-classical economy, and
the mechanisms through which they have worked have been
those that would not operate in a neo-classical world. The
evidence is that UK growth has been strongly influenced by
the expansion of demand and output actually achieved.
There is no support for the argument that UK growth has
been governed by the exogenously given growth of factor
inputs and productivity, and also no evidence that inefficiency has been a cause of slow growth. Thus the general
objection to the Conservative strategy is that it depends on
the properties of a theoretical model whose account of the
causes and mechanisms of growth bears almost no resemb-
lance to what can be observed in the post-war growth record
of the UK economy. The specific objection is that if the
mechanisms of UK growth operate now and in the future as
they have done in the past, the gains to growth from a policy
of lower inflation and freer competition will be (1) small and
(2) swamped by the damage to productive capacity and
growth inflicted by deflation which the policy itself requires.

Many advocates of current policy would probably not dis-
agree too strongly with this conclusion, but would insist that
the mechanisms that will operate will not be those of the
past. In particular they would claim (or hope) that the Government's measures for liberalization and freer competition
will so transform the structure of institutions and attitudes in
the UK that a neo-classical strategy for faster growth will be
appropriate and effective. A difficulty with this view is that it

exposes its supporters to the charge of inconsistency. How is it that the Government is powerless to bring about a change in the growth of output (and even in the level of output in the short run) attained within a given economic and social structure, but powerful enough to transform the structure of economic institutions and social attitudes? There has been no explicit discussion of this question in the current policy debate. The implicit answer seems to be that the required transformation does not involve a laborious erection of alternative structures starting from scratch, but the much less demanding task of releasing powerful latent forces which will benefit all. The belief seems to be that behind the obstructions erected by trade unions and monopoly producers in the private and public sectors there is a vigorous competitive economy the release of which will bring benefits to the great majority of the population. This is not a claim which can be directly tested, and even if it could empirical evidence would not settle the matter one way or the other for there are also judgements about the conditions of political freedom and equality at stake at this level of the debate. One observation of fact is, however, worth making. This claim about the nature of the transformation implies a rather thin explanation of non-competitive institutions. If such institutions are so obviously degenerate how have they become so prominent a feature of the structure of economies such as the UK? A more convincing interpretation, which incidentally is much more consistent with the ideas of economic theory, is that non-competitive institutions have developed as collective bodies serving interests which the relevant memberships see as legitimate but unattainable in a competitive system. This implies that non-competitive structures are an integral part of an economy such as the UK rather than an extraneous feature of it, and that the mechanisms of growth are much less manipulable than the advocates of current policy seem to suppose. Some supporters of the Conservative strategy might agree with this but insist, as Government spokesmen have repeatedly insisted, that the present policy, although difficult, is one to which there is no viable alternative.

An alternative strategy

The case for an alternative to the Conservative strategy based on a policy of expansion has been argued by Blake and Ormerod (1980) and, consistently and most forcefully, by the Cambridge Economic Policy Group. An up-to-date statement of the CEPG position can be found in chapters 1, 2 and 3 of the April 1980 issue of the *Cambridge Economic Policy Review*. The explanation of UK growth offered in this book supports these arguments. The analysis of the previous chapters provides no basis whatsoever for the claim that only the policy now in force offers any prospect of success. On the contrary, this analysis points to a direction for growth policy which offers better prospects than that which is currently being followed. The requirement for faster growth is a steady and sustained expansion of demand based on a reversal of previous trends in the trade performance of the UK in manufactured goods. A policy designed to bring this about has more chance of success than current policy for the simple reason that, in contrast to current policy, it would be aimed directly at those factors which have been most important in governing UK growth in the past, and would not include measures whose direct effect on growth is adverse.

It is not difficult to describe the features and circumstances of faster growth. Improving trade performance and expanding demand will interact with the growth of actual output and potential output in a self-reinforcing relationship. The problem of policy is to know how to get there from where we are without incurring prohibitive costs. The task of policy is to map out and negotiate the transition path. As trade performance will not improve spontaneously the stimulus to demand along the transition path must first come from domestic sources, that is from a reversal of the present fiscal and monetary strategy. Only a very crude understanding of the trade–demand hypothesis would support the view that an expansion of demand is all that is required to solve the problem of growth. There are two reasons why an expansion of demand, although necessary for faster growth, would not be sufficient. First, the existing supply of resources will set a limit to the expansion of domestic production in the short-run period before induced increases in investment and productivity begin to set in motion the cumulative forces of growth. This means that the expansion of demand will draw in imports and run foul of a growing balance of payments deficit at some point in the transitional phase. Some economists would also argue that an expansionist policy will for the same reason run straight into a problem of accelerating inflation. Whether the inflation rate would in fact be increased, unaffected or even reduced by a fiscal and monetary expansion is an extremely controversial issue which is far too large to be explored in any detail here. The greatest distance lies between those who see the excessive expansion of demand as the primary cause of inflation and those who argue that a demand expansion which provides some increase in living standards will reduce the extent to which trade unions fail to achieve their wage targets and thus ease the cost pressures which act on inflation regardless of the pressure of demand.[3] What can be said is that it is not clear than an expansion of demand would much worsen inflation but it would sooner or later worsen the balance of payments. The second problem is that it is hard to see that the effects of an expansion of demand on investment and productivity would by themselves be sufficiently powerful to halt and reverse the strongly adverse trends in the trade performance of the UK. The effects of an expansion on investment and productivity will do something to improve the design and quality of what is already being produced, but what is required is a massive reallocation of resources into the production of new manufactured goods which will be in demand in world markets. Although such a reallocation will never be effected in a slump only an extreme optimist would expect that an expansion of demand will be sufficient to achieve it. The conclusion to be drawn from these two points is that an expansion of domestic demand will not result in a sustainable improvement in trade performance and growth unless it is supported by a set of measures designed to (1) protect the balance of payments, and (2) restructure manufacturing production.

The question of protection for the balance of payments has been given rather more attention than it deserves by the controversy provoked by the proposals of the Cambridge Economic Policy Group for import controls.[4] The basic case for protection through import controls is that the alternative of devaluation will be ineffective due to the sluggish response of trade flows to changes in relative prices. The factors making for a lack of responsiveness are those referred to in chapter 6, namely the pricing behaviour of firms and the wage resistance offered by trade unions. Many of those who reject the Cambridge proposals do so from the conviction that effective devaluation is possible. Thus the dispute about import controls versus devaluation is an argument about workable forms of protection in which no great issues of theory and principle are at stake. Indeed the Cambridge advocates of import controls would prefer the devaluation alternative if it could be made effective by a successful incomes policy, but their belief is that this is not possible.

It is unfortunate that the issue of how to protect the balance of payments has occupied such a large part of the debate amongst the expansionists. The purpose of devaluation or import controls is to protect the expansionist strategy during the transitional phase; but neither device will correct the more fundamental problem of the chronic disability apparent in the trade performance of the UK manufacturing sector. Less attention has been given to how the trend of falling exports and rising import penetration will actually be reversed. Some hope seems to be pinned on a 'demand side miracle' whereby the trading base of the economy will be transformed by induced increases in investment and productivity; but such a result is much more than can reasonably be hoped for. This means that measures to expand demand and protect the balance of payments will only stand a fair chance of success if they are introduced in a package which includes an active industrial strategy. The industrial strategy will require

> (1) a more detailed understanding than is presently available of why many UK manufacturing industries have surrendered prominent positions in world markets;

(2) an identification of those manufactured goods with a high income elasticity of demand in world markets, taking into account the comparative advantage of newly industrialized economies in those manufactures the production of which can be automated on a large scale and made routine; and
(3) in the light of (1) and (2) whatever combination of public finance, control and ownership will be most effective in reallocating resources in UK manufacturing.

As the reallocation will need to be highly selective, the most appropriate strategy would be one in which a central position is given to public investment in manufacturing rather than to general fiscal incentives. This will require a substantial expansion of the funding and activities of the National Enterprise Board or the establishment of a similar body. The implication of this element of the strategy is that the initial stimulus to domestic demand should be largely devoted to public investment in manufacturing.

The standard objection to proposals for public investment in the private sector is that resources directed in this way will be wasted, or at least allocated less efficiently than by the market. There is, however, often a false standard of comparison in this objection. The entrepreneur of neo-classical theory may be much more efficient than the political administrators who would implement such a policy; but this is not the choice which is available. The actual alternatives are a chronically inefficient private manufacturing sector and a less than perfect political mechanism. Any public policy may be inefficient, but the investment policy proposed here would have to be not merely inefficient but massively inept to produce results worse than those shown over recent decades in the trade performance of the UK private manufacturing sector.

An objection to the whole package of measures proposed above is that the expansion of manufacturing it envisages will, for reasons outlined in the previous chapter, be inconsistent with the changes in the structure of the UK economy made inevitable by the discovery and exploitation of North

Sea oil. In fact there is very little real conflict on this issue. The apparent difficulty arises in part from the fact that a different standard of comparison is involved in the oil argument to that involved in the expansion argument. It is true by definition that UK non-oil manufacturing (and all other non-oil sectors) will account for a smaller proportion of GDP than they would have done had North Sea oil not been discovered or left in the sea bed. It is also true that the mechanisms of the economy – including changes in the exchange rate – may operate in such a way as to reduce the absolute size of the manufacturing sector below what it would have been had there been no oil. As there is no reason to suppose that this outcome can or should be avoided, a policy of reflation will expand the manufacturing sector to a size smaller than that it would have attained had there been no oil. However, the manufacturing sector will in this case be much larger than it is now and much larger than it will be if present policies are persisted with. Thus the growth rate of manufacturing under a policy of expansion will be significantly greater than it has been and will be under present policies, although less than it would have been without oil. The distance between the two arguments is further reduced if the finite life of North Sea oil is taken into account. Oil production from current discoveries is forecast to fall in the 1990s, after which time the economy will become more dependent on the trade performance of the manufacturing sector. It is therefore vital for growth in the long run that the reconstruction of UK manufacturing is not seriously impaired by the economic effects of North Sea oil. The contraction of manufacturing relative to the non-oil case can be smaller rather than greater and it is important that steps are taken to see that this happens. This means that the resources and tax revenues provided by oil should be used to regenerate the domestic manufacturing sector rather than to boost private consumption or investment abroad.

It will be objected that the proposals in this chapter are based on an incomplete understanding of the fundamental problem of trade performance, and that due to the world recession the scope for unilateral reflation is much less than the proposals suppose and require. It is perfectly true that the understanding of the immediate causes of UK growth offered in this book does not provide a complete explanation of it and that there is a limit to what can be done; but these facts are not good reasons for doing nothing in the present situation and still less do they justify a policy which is likely to make things worse.

Notes

1. For a fuller analysis of the depressive impulses felt in all advanced economies during the 1970s see Maddison (1980).
2. For a full statement of Conservative policies for growth see Sir Geoffrey Howe's letter to the House of Commons Treasury and Civil Service Committee in Cmnd. 450 (1980).
3. For a very good review of the argument see Allsopp and Joshi (1980).
4. See again Allsopp and Joshi (1980) for a review of the controversy on import controls.

Bibliography

Aldcroft, D. H. and Feron, P. (eds) (1969) *Economic Growth in 20th Century Britain* London, Macmillan.

Allsopp, C. and Joshi, V. (1980) 'Alternative Strategies for the UK' *National Institute Economic Review*, February 1980.

Bacon, R. and Eltis, W. (1978) *Britain's Economic Problem: Too Few Producers* 2nd edition, London, Macmillan.

Bacon, R. and Eltis, W. A. (1979) 'The Measurement of the Non-Market Sector and its Influence: A Reply to Hadjimatheou and Skouras' *Economic Journal* June 1979.

Ball, R. J. (ed.) (1973) *The International Linkage of Economic Models* Amsterdam, North-Holland.

Ball, R. J. Eaton, J. R. and Steuer, M. D. (1966) 'The Relationship Between United Kingdom Export Performance in Manufactures and the Internal Pressure of Demand' *Economic Journal* September 1966.

Bank of England (1977) *Bank of England Quarterly Bulletin* June 1977.

Beckerman, W. (1965) *The British Economy in 1975* Cambridge, The National Institute of Economic and Social Research and Cambridge University Press.

Beckerman, W. (ed.) (1979) *Slow Growth in Britain* Oxford, Oxford University Press.

Blackaby, F. (ed.) (1979) *De-Industrialization* London, National Institute of Economic and Social Research and Heinemann Educational Books.

Blake, D. and Ormerod, P. (eds) (1980) *The Economics of Prosperity* London, Grant McIntyre.

Branson, W. H. and Litvack, J. M. (1976) *Macroeconomics* New York, Harper and Row.

Brown, C. J. F. and Sheriff, T. D. (1979) 'De-industrialization: a Background Paper' in Blackaby (1979).

Byers, J. F. (1976) 'The Supply of Labour' in Heathfield (1976).

Caves, R. E. (1968) *Britain's Economic Prospects* London, The Brookings Institution and George Allen & Unwin.

Cmnd 450 (1980) House of Commons Treasury and Civil Service

118

Committee Session 1979–80 'Memoranda on Monetary Policy and Public Expenditure' London, HMSO.

Cmnd 7794 (1980) *Engineering our Future* (Report of The Committee of Enquiry into the Engineering Profession) London, HMSO.

Cmnd 7937 (1980) Committee to Review the Functioning of Financial Institutions, *Report* London, HMSO.

Connell, D. (1979) *The UK's Performance in Export markets — Some Evidence from International Trade Data* London, NEDO Discussion Paper 6.

Cornwall, J. (1976) 'Diffusion, Convergence and Kaldor's Laws' *Economic Journal* June 1976.

Cornwall, J. (1977a) *Modern Capitalism: Its Growth and Transformation* Oxford, Martin Robertson.

Cornwall, J. (1977b) 'The Relevance of Dual Models for Analysing Developed Capitalist Economies' *Kyklos* Fasc. 1, 1977.

Coutts, K. J. Godley, W. A. H. and Nordhaus, W. D. (1978) *Industrial Pricing in the United Kingdom* Cambridge, University of Cambridge Department of Applied Economics, Monograph 26.

Cripps, T. F. and Tarling, R. J. (1973) *Growth in Advanced Capitalist Economies 1950–1970* Cambridge, University of Cambridge Department of Applied Economics Occasional Paper 40.

CPRS (1975) *The Future of The British Car Industry* London, Central Policy Review Staff, HMSO.

Denison, E. F. (1967) *Why Growth Rates Differ* Washington, The Brookings Institution.

Denison, E. F. (1968) 'Economic Growth' in Caves (1968).

Eltis, W. (1979a) 'How Rapid Public Sector Growth can Undermine the Growth of the National Product' in W. Beckerman (1979).

Eltis, W. (1979b) 'Comment' in Blackaby (1979).

Enoch, C. A. (1978) 'Measures of Competitiveness in International Trade' *Bank of England Quarterly Bulletin* June 1978.

Fei, J. C. and Ranis, G. (1964) *Development of the Labour Surplus Economy* Homewood Ill., Irwin.

Feldstein, M. S. and Fleming, J. S. (1971) 'Tax Policy, Corporate Saving and Investment Behaviour in Britain' *Review of Economic Studies* October 1971.

Floud, R. (1979) *An Introduction to Quantitative Methods For Historians* 2nd edition, London, Methuen.

Forsyth, P. J. and Kay, J. A. (1980) 'The Economic Implications of North Sea Oil Revenues' *Fiscal Studies* July 1980.

Fromm, G. (ed.) (1971) *Tax Incentives and Capital Spending* Washington, Brookings Institution.

Gamble, A. and Walton, P. (1976) *Capitalism in Crisis, Inflation and the State* London, Macmillan.

Glyn, A. and Sutcliffe, B. (1972) *British Capitalism, Workers and the Profits Squeeze* London, Penguin Books.

Gomulka, S. (1971) *Inventive Activity, Diffusion and the Stages of Economic Growth* Aarhus, Institute of Economics.

Gomulka, S. (1979) 'Britain's Slow Industrial Growth, Increasing Inefficiency Versus Slow Rate of Technical Change' in Beckerman (1979).

Haache, G. (1979) *The Theory of Economic Growth: An Introduction* London, Macmillan.

Hadjimatheou, G. and Skouras, A. (1979) 'Britain's Economic Problem: The Growth of the Non-Market Sector' *Economic Journal* June 1979.

Hahn, F. and Neild, R. (1980) 'Monetarism: why Mrs Thatcher should beware' *The Times* 25 February 1980.

Harrod, R. (1933) *International Economics* London, Nisbet.

Harrod, R. (1967) 'Assessing the Trade Returns' *Economic Journal* September 1967.

Heathfield, D. F. (1976) *Topics in Applied Macroeconomics* New York, Academic Press.

Heathfield, D. F. and Hilton, K. (eds) (1970) *The Econometric Study of United Kingdom* London, Macmillan.

Hines, A. G. and Catephores, G. (1970) 'Investment in UK Manufacturing Industry 1956–1967' in Heathfield and Hilton (1970).

Houthakker H. S. and Magee, S. P. (1969) 'Income and Price Elasticities in World Trade' *Review of Economics and Statistics* May 1968.

Hughes, J. J. and Thirwall, A. P. (1977) 'Trends and Cycles in Import Penetration in the UK' *Oxford Bulletin of Economics and Statistics* November 1977.

Institute for Fiscal Studies (1977) *Fiscal Policy and Labour Supply* London.

Jackson, P. M. (1977) 'The Growth of Public Sector Employment' in Institute for Fiscal Studies (1977).

Junankar, P. N. (1970) 'The Relationship between Investment and Spare Capacity in the UK 1957–1966' *Economica* August 1970.

Junankar, P. N. (1972) *Investment: Theories and Evidence* London, Macmillan.

Junz, H. and Rhomberg, R. (1965) 'Prices and Export Performance of Industrialized Countries 1953–1963' *IMF Staff Papers* July 1965.

Kaldor, N. (1966) *Causes of the Slow Rate of Growth of the United Kingdom, an Inaugural Lecture* Cambridge, Cambridge University Press.

Kaldor, N. (1967) *Strategic Factors in Economic Development* New York, School of Industrial and Labour Relations, Cornell University.

Kaldor, N. (1968) 'Productivity and Growth in Manufacturing: A Reply' *Economica* November 1968.

Kaldor, N. (1975a) 'What is Wrong with Economic Theory' *Quarterly Journal of Economics* August 1975.

Kaldor, N. (1975b) 'Economic Growth and the Verdoorn Law: a Comment on Mr. Rowthorn's Article' *Economic Journal* December 1975.

Kaldor, N. (1978a) 'Capitalism and Industrial Development: Some Lessons from Britain's Experience' in N. Kaldor *Further Essays on Applied Economics* London, Duckworth, 1978.

Kaldor, N. (1978b) 'The Effect of Devaluations on Trade in Manufactures' in N. Kaldor *Further Essays on Applied Economics* London, Duckworth, 1978.

Kaldor, N. (1980) Letter to *New Statesman* 14 March 1980.

Kennedy, K. A. (1971) *Productivity and Industrial Growth, the Irish Experience* Oxford, Oxford University Press.

Kilpatrick, A. and Lawson, T. (1980) 'On the Nature of Industrial Decline in the UK' *Cambridge Journal of Economics* March 1980.

Krause, L. B. (1968) 'British Trade Performance' in Caves (1968).

Labour Party (1976) *Banking and Finance*.

Maddison, A. (1964) *Economic Growth in the West* London, George Allen & Unwin.

Maddison, A. (1977) 'Phases of Capitalist Development' *Banca Nazionale del Lavore Quarterly Review* June 1977.

Maddison, A. (1979) 'Long Run Dynamics of Productivity Growth' in Beckerman (1979).

Maddison, A. (1980) 'Western Economic Performance in the 1970s: A Perspective and Assessment' *Banca Nazionale Del Lavore Quarterly Review* September 1980.

Major, R. L. (1968) 'Note on Britain's Share of World Trade in Manufactures 1954–1966' *National Institute Economic Review* May 1968.

Manison, L. G. (1978) 'Some Factors Influencing the United Kingdom's Economic Performance' *IMF Staff Papers* December 1978.

Matthews, R. C. O. (1973) 'Foreign Trade and British Economic Growth' *Scottish Journal of Political Economy* November 1973.

Minford, P. (1980) 'The Nature and Purpose of UK Macro-economic Models' *Three Banks Review* March 1980.

NEDO (1975) *Finance for Investment* London, National Economic Development Office.

Nobay, A. R. (1970) 'Forecasting Manufacturing Investment – Some Preliminary Results' *National Institute Economic Review* May 1970.

OECD (1961) *Manpower Statistics 1950–1960* Paris, OECD.

OECD (1969) *Labour Force Statistics 1956–1967* Paris, OECD.

OECD (1970) *The Growth of Output 1960–1980* Paris, OECD.

OECD (1976) *Labour Force Statistics 1963–1974* Paris, OECD.

OECD (1977) *Towards Full Employment and Price Stability: A Report to the OECD by a Group of Independent Experts* Paris, OECD.

OECD (1980) *The United Kingdom* Paris, OECD Economic Survey.

Panić, M. (1975) 'Why the UK's Propensity to Import is High' *Lloyds Bank Review* January 1975.

Panić, M. and Rajan, A. H. (1979) *Product Changes in Industrial Countries' Trade* 2nd edition, London, NEDO.

Panić, M. and Seward, T. (1966) 'The Problem of UK Exports' *Bulletin of Oxford Institute of Economics and Statistics* February 1966.

Panić, M. and Vernon, K. (1975) 'Major Factors Behind Investment Decisions in British Manufacturing Industry' *Oxford Bulletin of Economics and Statistics* August 1975.

Parikh, A. (1978) 'Differences in Growth Rates and Kaldor's Laws' *Economica* February 1978.

Pratten, C. F. and Atkinson, A. G. (1976) 'The Use of Manpower in British Manufacturing' *Department of Employment Gazette* June 1976.

Purdy, D. (1976) 'British Capitalism Since the War, Part One – Origin of the Crisis; Part Two – Decline and Prospects' *Marxism Today* September and October 1976.

Rowthorn, R. E. (1975a) 'What Remains of Kaldor's Law?' *Economic Journal* March 1975.

Rowthorn, R. E. (1975b) 'A Reply to Lord Kaldor's Comment' *Economic Journal* December 1975.

Samuel, J. M., Groves, R. E. V. and Goddard, C. S. (1975) *Company Finance in Europe* London, The Institute of Chartered Accountants.

Sargent, J. R. (1979) 'UK Performance in Services' in Blackaby (1979).

Savage, D. (1978) 'The Channels of Monetary Influence: A Survey of the Empirical Evidence' *National Institute Economic Review* February 1978.

Singh, A. (1977) 'UK Industry and the World Economy: a Case of De-industrialization' *Cambridge Journal of Economics* June 1977.

Smyth, D. J. (1968) 'Stop–Go and the United Kingdom Exports of Manufactures' *Bulletin of the Oxford Institute of Economics and Statistics* February 1968.

Smyth, D. J. and Briscoe, G. (1969) 'Investment Plans and Realizations in UK Manufacturing' *Economica* August 1969.

Taplin, G. R. (1973) 'A Model of World Trade' in Ball (1973).

Tarling, R. J. and Cripps, T. F. (1973) *Growth in Advanced Capitalist Economies 1950–1970* Cambridge, University of Cambridge Department of Applied Economics Occasional Paper 40.

Thatcher, A. R. (1979) 'Labour Supply and Employment Trends' in Blackaby (1979).

Thirwall, A. P. (1980) *Balance of Payments Theory and the United Kingdom Experience* London, Macmillan.

Thirwall, A. P. and Thirwall, G. (1979) 'Factors Governing the Growth of Labour Productivity' *Research in Population and Economics* Autumn 1979.

HM Treasury (1978) 'The International Competitiveness of UK Manufactured Goods' in *Economic Progress Report* February 1978.

United Nations (1970) *Economic Survey of Europe 1969 Part 1* New York, United Nations.

Vaciago, G. (1975) 'Increasing Returns and Growth in Advanced Economies: a Re-evaluation' *Oxford Economic Papers* July 1975.

Verdoorn, P. J. (1949) 'Fattori che regolano lo sviluppo della produttivitá del lavoro' *L'Industria* 1949. Translated in Thirwall and Thirwall (1979).

Whiting, A. (1976) 'An International Comparison of the Instability of Economic Growth' *Three Banks Review* March 1976.

Wilson, T. (1969) 'Instability and Growth: An International Comparison' in Aldcroft and Fearon (1969).

Index